# Magazine Production

3

070.572 WH1

# LEARNING.
## ••••••••••••services

01209 616182

616259.

### Cornwall College Camborne
*Learning Centre - HE*

This resource is to be returned on or before the last date stamped below. To renew items please contact the Centre

3 issues – 2010

## Three Week Loan

-8 DEC 2010  RETURNED

26 APR 2011  RETURNED

27 FEB 2013

19 MAR 2013  RETURNED

*Magazine* from init title as p an overvi a magazi and prepa

*Magazine* and Nort establishi the Perio understar

*Magazine*

- an
- exp the
- hov
- gui fea
- inf
- leg
- a c

**Jason WI** with a sp has 15 ye interest in II and B2B titles. He is the author of numerous academic books and articles including *The Cyberspace Handbook* (2004) and *Web Production for Writers and Journalists* (2002).

CP035285

CORNWALL COLLEGE

# Media Skills

SERIES EDITOR: RICHARD KEEBLE, LINCOLN UNIVERSITY
SERIES ADVISERS: WYNFORD HICKS AND JENNY McKAY

The *Media Skills* series provides a concise and thorough introduction to a rapidly changing media landscape. Each book is written by media and journalism lecturers or experienced professionals and is a key resource for a particular industry. Offering helpful advice and information and using practical examples from print, broadcast and digital media, as well as discussing ethical and regulatory issues, *Media Skills* books are essential guides for students and media professionals.

**English for Journalists**
3rd edition
*Wynford Hicks*

**Writing for Journalists**
*Wynford Hicks with Sally Adams,
Harriett Gilbert and Tim Holmes*

**Interviewing for Radio**
*Jim Beaman*

**Web Production for Writers and Journalists**
2nd edition
*Jason Whittaker*

**Ethics for Journalists**
*Richard Keeble*

**Scriptwriting for the Screen**
*Charlie Moritz*

**Interviewing for Journalists**
*Sally Adams, with an introduction
and additional material by
Wynford Hicks*

**Researching for Television and Radio**
*Adèle Emm*

**Reporting for Journalists**
*Chris Frost*

**Subediting for Journalists**
*Wynford Hicks and Tim Holmes*

**Designing for Newspapers and Magazines**
*Chris Frost*

**Writing for Broadcast Journalists**
*Rick Thompson*

**Freelancing for Television and Radio**
*Leslie Mitchell*

**Programme Making for Radio**
*Jim Beaman*

**Magazine Production**
*Jason Whittaker*

Find more details of current *Media Skills* books and forthcoming titles at
**www.producing.routledge.com**

# Magazine
# Production

Jason Whittaker

Routledge
Taylor & Francis Group

LONDON AND NEW YORK

First published 2008
by Routledge
2 Park Square, Milton Park, Abingdon, Oxon OX14 4RN

Simultaneously published in the USA and Canada
by Routledge
270 Madison Ave, New York, NY 10016

*Routledge is an imprint of the Taylor & Francis Group, an informa business*

© 2008 Jason Whittaker

Typeset in Goudy and Scala Sans by
Florence Production Ltd, Stoodleigh, Devon
Printed and bound in Great Britain by
TJ International Ltd, Padstow, Cornwall

*British Library Cataloguing in Publication Data*
A catalogue record for this book is available from the British Library

*Library of Congress Cataloging in Publication Data*
Whittaker, Jason, 1969–
    Magazine production / Jason Whittaker.
        p. cm. — (Media skills)
    Includes bibliographical references and index.
    1. Periodicals—Publishing—Handbooks, manuals, etc.
    2. Magazine design—Handbooks, manuals, etc.   I. Title.
    Z286.P4W48 2008
    070.5'72—dc22

ISBN10: 0–415–43519–6 (hbk)
ISBN10: 0–415–43520–X (pbk)

ISBN13: 978–0–415–43519–2 (hbk)
ISBN13: 978–0–415–43520–8 (pbk)

To Sam, for all her patience

# Contents

# Illustrations

## Figures

## Tables

# Introduction

Magazines fill our daily lives. Often we encounter them casually – as filler when we are waiting for an appointment, or something to read while travelling by train. At other times, they are the focus for interests, hobbies and our professional life, something that we subscribe to or actively seek out because they are the best source of information on a particular subject.

Despite the proliferation of other media, such as online technologies and digital television, magazines have simply never been as popular, with much of the success of the format being due to the proliferation of titles capable of reaching niche audiences. While there are dozens of television channels and hundreds of newspapers in the UK, for example, there are more than 8,000 magazines, although most of these are only read by a small section of the population.

Publications fall into two broad categories: those aimed at the consumer and those which are designed for professionals or people working in an industry or business. In addition, there are other periodicals produced for an academic or highly specialised market, such as science and medicine, or the arts and humanities. These tend to have very restricted circulations and very little, if any, advertising. As such, they are not covered in the following chapters which focus, instead, on commercial titles.

This book concentrates on magazine production, the skills needed to create a magazine in terms of editorial, design and printing. However, it also aims to provide the reader with a background to some elements of magazine publishing, and outline the main players in the UK and worldwide market.

Different chapters deal with the role of the publisher and the importance of advertising, as well as various elements of magazine business such as distribution, circulation and marketing. Although these would not necessarily be immediately important for students working on a magazine for college or university, anyone who hopes to break into the magazine industry should have a solid understanding of the business side of publishing. What is more, editors need to deal with publishers, advertising sales teams, marketing managers and circulation directors on a regular basis, and the demands of these various departments all feed into the production of a commercial title.

An important aim of this book, then, is to introduce the reader to key terminology, contexts and practices in the magazine industry, explaining the differences between consumer and business-to-business (B2B) sectors, the financial requirements and business of publishing. The main part of the book also works through the abilities and skills that are required to take a magazine from initial concept to finished product.

Chapter 1 provides an overview of the magazine industry, tracing its history and looking in some detail at the types of publications on offer and the main publishers. There is also an introduction to the role of the Periodical Publishers Association, the main industry body for magazines.

Chapter 2 concentrates on the business of publishing, looking in particular at the role of the publisher and how he or she relates to other departments on a typical commercial magazine. Although the main focus of this book is magazine production, some understanding of how other departments, such as advertising, work will be useful for those seeking a job in magazines.

Similarly, knowing how titles are distributed and sold is extremely important to the editor. Chapter 3 discusses the importance of creating a solid circulation through newsstand sales and subscriptions, and also considers how magazine promotion works through such things as media packs, which publications use to connect with advertisers.

The next three chapters deal with the production process proper, beginning with editorial and copy in Chapter 4. After discussing the role of the editor, and how a typical magazine editorial department is structured, this chapter goes on to discuss the type of planning cycles that need to be put in place to make a title successful. It also considers the main types of article that appear in publications – news, features and reviews – with a brief account of the role of commissioning editors.

A good magazine does not simply consist of text, however, so Chapter 5 looks at the role of the art editor and the importance of good design in creating compelling publications. This chapter concentrates on typography, colour and graphics (photography and illustration), and how these are used to create a visual object that will appeal to readers.

Chapter 6 brings together copy and art in terms of page design and final production. As well as considering what part a production editor plays in the day-to-day running of a magazine, and looking at the role of new technologies in page design, this chapter provides an overview of the final stages of getting a title into print and finished for distribution.

In Chapter 7, readers are given a concise overview of the main legal and ethical challenges that face magazine editors and journalists, in particular libel and copyright. Here readers will also find information about some of the professional bodies that affect journalism in the UK, such as the National Union of Journalists and the Press Complaints Commission.

Finally, although this is a book that concentrates on print magazines, the concluding chapter takes a brief look at some of the ways in which publications are using the web and new media to engage with their audiences in different ways.

The book includes a glossary of useful terms for magazine publishing, as well as a bibliography and a list of helpful web sites.

# 1
# Magazines and their markets

## Magazines and print media

Magazines provide the most diverse form of print media available today in terms of content, markets and formats, and are nearly as old as the other type of periodical regularly consumed, newspapers. In terms of their physical format, although most of the titles we see on the newsstand are approximately A4 in size, a few may be A5 and in terms of volume and paper quality they can vary enormously.

It is with regard to markets and content, however, that the real range of magazines can be seen. From weekly news digest titles and monthly general men's and women's magazines, to specialist titles for particular consumer and professional interests, before the rise of the Internet no other medium focused on specific niche markets to the same degree.

Magazines are often referred to as periodicals, and it is the regular nature of their appearance – not daily like most national and many regional newspapers, but weekly, monthly or at other set times during the year – that in many ways defines their status. As the majority of titles tend to be much more specific than newsprint, the calendar of events for such things as fashion shows, new car launches or the holiday seasons punctuate the ebb and flow of information that we have come to expect from the glossies.

## Types of magazine

To stretch the definition of magazines to some degree, some would probably also include newsletters in this category (particularly as an increasing number of these include photography and can be printed on high-grade paper stock), although others would deny them the status of being magazines because of the highly targeted nature of their content and also because subscriptions to professional newsletters are often extremely expensive, far out of the price range of the average magazine reader.

One major development over the past decade, and one that will be considered towards the end of this book, is the rise of the electronic or e-zine. Often combining a similar combination of image and text as is found in the glossies, online e-zines such as *Slate* (www.slate.com) or *Wall Street Journal Online* (http://online.wsj.com) have become increasingly respected in certain areas for providing high-quality journalism and content.

Of course, what is very different to this type of publication is the ability to provide multimedia that brings together audio and video, part of the process of convergence that is affecting media around the world – and with which, it must be noted, some traditional publishers are struggling to come to terms as they see their audiences shift online.

At the other end of the scale, the web has extended interest in zines, or fanzines, which, as well as appearing in electronic format, are also enjoying something of a revival in print. In contrast to professional e-zines, fanzines and comics will not be discussed in this book.

## The popularity of magazines

Despite the growth of the World Wide Web, new media and technologies have not diminished the popularity of magazines. Traditionally, magazines have tended to be divided into two types: consumer and specialised business titles, the latter once referred to as trade magazines but more often now as business-to-business, or B2B. Consumer magazines will carry a great deal of advertising and be available in a wide number of outlets, while B2B titles are usually only available to a restricted number of readers – something that will be considered in much more detail in Chapter 3.

According to British Rates and Data (BRAD), the total number of magazines published in the UK in 2006 was 8,558, of which 3,445 were consumer magazines and 5,113 aimed at the B2B sector. This represented a 21 per cent increase since 1993, when the total was 6,618. In the USA, about 1,000 companies publish magazines with a combined annual revenue of more than $40 billion in 2005 according to Business Wire although fewer than 200 have circulations higher than half a million.

In the UK, the Advertising Association observes that advertising revenues for magazines increased from £499 million in 1994 to £827 million in 2005 for consumer titles, and from £785 million to just over £1 billion for B2B in the same period. Of course, these figures are put into the shade by Internet advertising, which grew literally from nothing to be worth nearly £1.4 billion (and which is still growing rapidly); likewise, taking that ten-year figure alone tends to obscure the fact that after a huge growth in the late 1990s B2B revenues have declined slightly.

Nevertheless, it is clear that magazine publishing in the UK, as elsewhere in Europe and the US, remains a healthy business, especially when compared to the overall slow decline of regional and national newspapers. During that period, the quality of design and print has also continued to improve – if not always matched by equal improvements in editorial.

The National Readership Survey (NRS) reports that nearly 75 per cent of adults read a consumer magazine, a figure that rises to more than 80 per cent among 15–24-year-olds. Ever since they became a fixture of modern life at the end of the nineteenth century, part of the modern mass media that shaped our perceptions of the past 120 years, we have used magazines to develop our tastes, pursue our gossip, improve our professional life, and as a window on the world about us.

## The beginnings of magazines

Magazines in Western Europe first began to appear in substantial numbers during the early eighteenth century, although their format was closer to that of news sheets, pamphlets and books than what we would recognise as magazines today. The original meaning of the word as a store for a variety of goods indicates the most significant difference between early magazines and the first newspapers that were published in Britain during the seventeenth century.

Rather than being restricted to news, magazines quickly established themselves as a forum for gentlemen editors and writers to espouse their opinions on a whole range of subjects, such as fashion and literary taste as well as politics and religion.

The first English magazine is typically taken to be Daniel Defoe's *The Review* (1704–13), which began the year after Defoe had been imprisoned for criticising the Church of England. The purpose of *The Review*, issued as four pages of densely printed text with few illustrations, was to offer comment and satire on the state of the nation, but the most famous of these early journals were *The Tatler* (1709) and *The Spectator* (1711–14), which were edited respectively by Joseph Addison and Richard Steele and included articles by many famous literary contributors such as Alexander Pope and Jonathan Swift.

Addison and Steele pioneered the short, informal essay, the elegant precursor of the feature article, establishing a new role for the modern journalist in the first issue of *The Spectator*:

> I have observed, that a Reader seldom peruses a Book with Pleasure 'till he knows whether the Writer of it be a black or a fair Man, of a mild or cholerick Disposition, Married or a Batchelor, with other Particulars of the like nature, that conduce very much to the right Understanding of an Author … I have passed my latter Years in this City, where I am frequently seen in most publick Places, tho' there are not above half a dozen of my select Friends that know me. There is no place of Resort wherein I do not often make my appearance; sometimes I am seen thrusting my Head into a Round of Politicians at 'Will's' and listning with great Attention to the Narratives that are made in those little Circular Audiences. Sometimes I smoak a Pipe at 'Child's' and, while I seem attentive to nothing but the Post-Man, over-hear the Conversation of every Table in the Room … Thus I live in the World, rather as a Spectator of Mankind, than as one of the Species; by which means I have made my self a Speculative Statesman, Soldier, Merchant, and Artizan, without ever medling with any Practical Part in Life … In short, I have acted in all the parts of my Life as a Looker-on, which is the Character I intend to preserve in this Paper.
>
> (No. 1, 1 March 1711)

The figure of the objective (and, indeed, arrogant) spectator – committed to no party and capable of spotting the errors of any mere practitioner – was soon to become an established component of eighteenth-century literary and political journalism. The growth of a bourgeois public sphere

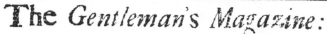

Figure 1.1 *The Gentleman's Magazine*, 1748

in London, centred on the new wealth of a capitalist empire, brought with it new opportunities and new anxieties.

Under a feudal system, rank and custom had been clearly defined by birth and ownership of land, but in this new order the role of gentleman was increasingly demarcated (and, for many, increasingly defiled) by wealth alone. For the *nouveau riches*, lacking centuries of tradition on how to behave, literary publications such as *The Spectator* provided necessary instruction on what to do in public.

One clear example of the significance of this new genre was *The Gentleman's Magazine*. Founded in 1731 by Edward Cave, it was one of the most successful magazines ever issued, not ceasing publication until 1907. Cave's original intention had been to provide a monthly digest of news and commentary, and the early issues of his title were a rich miscellany of information that no gentleman could afford to miss, including essays, poetry, extracts from new works and informative articles on religion and politics as well as endless lists on all topics from county sheriffs to bankrupts. Samuel Johnson was one of its more famous contributors, and Cave's canny business sense led to *The Gentleman's Magazine* being distributed throughout the English-speaking world.

For nearly two centuries after their initial appearance, magazines were largely the preserve of the upper classes. Relatively expensive to produce (certainly compared to later publications), late eighteenth- and early nineteenth-century titles such as *Blackwoods* and the *Edinburgh Review* tended to concentrate on literature and serious comment, with a rather austere format that changed little before the final decades of the nineteenth century.

## Technological innovation and the rise of mass media

The transformation of magazines into a mass commodity relied on two interrelated developments, innovations in technology and the rise of a mass media, both of which, in turn, depended on wider economic and social changes in Europe and North America.

Technological developments involved improvements in presswork, the process of transferring impressions to paper, and composition, creating readable type. The invention of lithography by Alois Senefelder in the late 1790s, and its subsequent enhancements in the following years, enabled the reproduction of text and image more cheaply than the laborious engraving techniques that had been used until that time.

By applying a waxy crayon to limestone, Senefelder could etch the plate surface with acid to leave a relief which was resistant to water: when the plate was dampened, ink could easily be applied and would not hold on the wet parts of the stone. Modern lithography uses photography to transfer an image to a metal plate or, with Computer-To-Plate (CTP) technology, the image is drawn by laser: in addition, the refinement of offset lithography, whereby the image from the plate is transferred to a rubber blanket before printing it onto paper, meant that images and text could be printed the correct way round.

While this process revolutionised presswork, composition was transformed radically by the invention of the Linotype machine by Ottmar Mergenthaler in 1886. Prior to this, individual letters of text were assembled by hand, but Mergenthaler's machine allowed a typesetter to retrieve a set of moulds, or matrices, of imprinted letters into which molten lead was poured to create a line of text. Because hand composition had been so time-consuming, newspapers were restricted to a few pages; this was less of an issue with magazines, which did not need to be produced daily, but all forms of journalism benefited from the invention of hot metal typesetting. Although eventually replaced by photographic lithography, the Linotype provided a huge advance in magazine production.

Printing presses themselves also underwent significant developments: the steam press, devised in 1812, enabled more than 1,000 pages to be printed per hour, while the rotary printing press (1833) increased this to a million copies of a page in a single day.

Technological innovations themselves, however, brought about by the improved manufacturing processes of industrialised societies, were not enough to create a mass media. The conditions that led to mass audiences included increased literacy rates (enabled in England, for example, by government-financed public education in 1870) and the increase in spare capital among the working classes that meant they could spend more on consumer commodities. By the final decade of the nineteenth century, entrepreneurial publishers were realising that they could take advantage of these new conditions.

In 1893, Samuel McClure released his literary and political *McClure's Magazine* at the low price of 15 cents, a title that published writers such as Arthur Conan Doyle and Rudyard Kipling, and which specialised in investigative journalism known as muckraking to its detractors (a phenomenon linked to the so-called sensationalist 'yellow journalism' that emerged during the circulation battles between Joseph Pulitzer and William Randolph Hearst in the late 1890s). Rival Frank Munsey cut the price of *Munsey's Magazine* to 10 cents, with both publishers seeking to attain higher profits through advertising rather than cover price.

**Figure 1.2** *Der Dada Magazine*, 1919

The contrast between this new breed of journalism and the genteel literary magazines became more pronounced at the turn of the century. As well as *Munsey's Magazine*, Frank Munsey had launched a title aimed at children called *Argosy*; costing 5 cents and comprising eight pages, it was not initially a success, but, relaunched as a title for adults at the end of the decade, it instituted the rise of the pulp magazines (so called because they were made from low-grade paper, in contrast to the 'slicks' aimed at more affluent readers).

From the 1920s through the 1950s, these pulp titles were published in increasing numbers and introduced what was, in some respects, a golden age of magazine publishing. While content was often of a quality that did not even match the paper it was printed on, the pulps were often great innovators in genre publishing, especially detective, horror and science fiction, providing a market for new writers in titles such as *Amazing Stories*, *Black Mask* and *Weird Tales*. The format was eventually to face decline from rising costs and competition from comics, television and cheap paperback novels.

## The design revolution

Technological innovations such as lithography meant that by 1900 magazines looked very different to the journals of a hundred years previously. Illustrations were now commonplace and the physical format of the magazine was similar to that of modern publications, with two further important developments being the invention of photography and the contribution of Modernism to the field of design.

By the final decade of the nineteenth century, photography had been in existence for nearly half a century, but the ability to mass produce photographs was extremely limited (for example, publishers would hire engravers to copy a photograph so that it could be transferred to print). The growing number of magazines in the early twentieth century fuelled the demand for more photographic illustrations, which in turn could be reproduced more easily by refinements to lithographic printing, while the development of lighter camera equipment such as the German-manufactured Ermanox and Leica compact cameras in the 1920s contributed to the growth of photojournalism.

Photography had been used to document important events since the American Civil War, but during the 1920s photo magazines increased in number. Publications such as the *Müncher Illustrierte Presse* and *Berliner Illustrierte Zeitung* began to publish a new style of spontaneous image, defined by Henri Cartier-Bresson as the 'decisive moment', which became enormously popular with the reading public. It was during the 1930s, however, with titles including *Life* (1936) in the USA and *Picture Post* (1938) in the UK, that photography became a staple of magazine production.

**Figure 1.3** *Life*, 1936

Alongside the important contribution of photography and photo-journalism, the format of magazine publishing was being revolutionised by the art of the avant garde. While the new artistic forms of cubism, Dadaism, futurism and surrealism appeared very far from the mass-consumerism of the muckraking or yellow press, many modern artists were fascinated by contemporary technology and culture. Initially, their experiments were confined to small-scale manifestos and journals, but the typographic and sophisticated graphic design pursued by publications such as *Der Dada*, *391* and *Minotaure* were taken up by advertisers and commercial magazine publishers in the inter-war period.

Ad agencies, which were first established during the 1890s, very quickly saw the appeal of new graphic formats, employing slogans, photography and bold imagery to grab the attention of consumers. As with other mass media formats (particularly poster art during the early twentieth century), advertising became extremely important to magazine publishers as a means to sell titles below cost. Successful magazine designers were often those who had also worked for advertisers, and as full page display advertising became the norm so editorial pages had to be more innovative to compete for the reader's attention.

It was during the inter-war period that one of the most important media companies of the twentieth century was created. *Time* was launched in 1923 by Briton Hadden and Henry Luce, the first weekly news magazine in the USA, and the pair established a publishing empire that would include *Fortune* (1930), *Life* (1936), *Sports Illustrated* (1954), and *People* (1974).

By the time of Luce's death in 1967, Time Inc. was worth $109 million and, following the merger with Warner Communications in 1990, became part of the world's largest media and entertainment company. This title was only recently surpassed by Google – although the new media company has a much lower turnover. Despite current downsizing of its portfolio of 150 titles, Time Warner is still the largest magazine publishing company in the US, with a market value of $78 billion on sales of $42 billion in 2005.

## The rise of the glossies

In the 1920s, pulp magazines were sometimes compared to the 'slicks', particularly fashion magazines such as *Vogue* that were printed on higher-quality paper with professional photography and full-colour on most, if not all, pages. It was not until the 1950s, however, that the full benefits of earlier innovations in design combined with a consumer boom after a period of post-war austerity to produce the contemporary glossy in all its glory.

In the 1930s, the first steps to recuperate the men's magazine market were taken by the publication of *Men Only* (1935) in the UK and *Esquire* (1933) in the US. As well as including that popular staple, the pin-up (only later to develop into more fully fledged pornography), these titles included articles, features and fashion pages designed for what publishers and advertisers saw as a sophisticated and affluent market.

By the middle of the century, men's magazines were seen as largely synonymous with pornography (for which *Playboy*, launched in 1953, bore some responsibility, although its publisher, Hugh Hefner, saw it as an extension of *Esquire* for which he had previously worked). Colour weekend supplements, such as those for *The Sunday Times*, attracted the advertising base that had previously read more general publications, and the entire market languished until the 1980s when titles such as *GQ* and *Arena* were imported to the UK from America.

However, the real shake-up of the market was seen in 1994, with the launch of *Loaded*: its irreverent attitude under the editorial lead of James Brown saw sales of over a quarter of a million by 1996, and it was quickly followed by a raft of titles such as *FHM* (bought by Emap from Tayvale) and *Maxim*. By 2006, sales had declined from a high point of 600,000 for *FHM* in 2003, but the general men's market – and its advertising base – had been well and truly established.

During the final decades of the twentieth century, the glossy look that had originally been pioneered by *Vogue*, *Esquire* and *Playboy* had now extended even into the trade and B2B sectors. In addition, the 1980s saw further technological developments which, in their own way, were as significant as the inventions of lithographic printing and photography.

The introduction of computers and desktop publishing saw radical changes to the ways that magazines were produced, with smaller teams capable of taking a title from initial conception to final print much more quickly and – once the technology had become widespread – more cheaply than ever before. By the early 1990s, it was predicted that magazine publishing would be opened up to a more democratic process; in one respect, while

**Figure 1.4** *Vogue*, 1950

it did become more profitable to engage in more and more niche publishing (particularly in the business market, which exploded from this period onwards), in reality the difficulties and costs of actually printing and distributing a magazine, as opposed simply to preparing copy and layouts, saw the consolidation of publishing houses continue apace into the twenty-first century.

## Markets and audiences

The development of magazines into a format that is instantly recognisable more or less anywhere in the world has been accompanied by a much greater segmentation of the magazine market. Unlike just about any other medium until the rise of the Internet and digital television, magazines are usually aimed at very specific, niche audiences, with readerships often numbering in the low thousands or tens of thousands.

## Consumer magazines

In terms of quantities of copies sold, consumer magazines dominate the newsstands. There are many more specialist trade and B2B titles, but the bestselling magazines are general men's and women's titles, as well as television guides, and leisure and domestic magazines. As Jenny McKay (2004) remarks: 'What most people immediately think about when magazines are mentioned are consumer publications, that is the ones which give readers information, advice and entertainment which relate to the time when they are not at work' (p. 26).

This is, of course, a wide definition. General entertainment titles are matched by those that aim to inform a more specialist (but non-professional) audience, such as those aimed at film buffs or car buyers. Although larger numbers of individual consumer magazines are sold in countries such as Japan and the US, for its size the UK has a considerably diverse range of titles – approximately 2,800 consumer magazines, compared to 3,200 in the US, with only about one fifth of the population. However, this diversity brings its own problems, making the market much more competitive in the UK. Added to this, consumer titles have declined in circulation: the Advertising Association (www.adassoc.org.uk) listed sales at about 1,400 million in 2004 compared to 2,100 million in 1970, although this does include a slight increase from a low point of 1,200 million in 1992.

## Women's magazines

The most financially successful category of consumer magazines, while women's magazines do not take up many of the top ten positions in terms of circulation (mainly filled by free subscription or supermarket magazines and TV guides), they do dominate the lists of sold titles. Ironically, as we have already seen when considering the history of magazines, the supremacy of titles aimed at women compared to general men's magazines has only been a relatively recent phenomenon.

Titles such as the *Ladies' Home Journal* began to appear for women in the nineteenth century, but it was during the twentieth century that these magazines exploded in circulation. In particular, they became an attractive prospect for advertisers who would target consumer products at readers.

The five top-selling monthlies aimed specifically at women for 2005 give some indication of the target audiences for publishers. *Good Housekeeping* is one of several magazines referred to as 'the Seven Sisters' in the USA; published by The National Magazine Company, it contains information on food, relationships and fashion as well as, of course, the home. *Cosmopolitan*, also from NatMags, is for many the classic women's magazine, although its focus on relationships, sex and careers belies some of the more investigative reporting of its earlier years; similar in look and feel are *Glamour* (Condé Nast) and *Marie Claire* (IPC). *Yours* (Emap Esprit, now fortnightly), by contrast, taps into the growing prosperity of the over-fifties market, including features on pensions and celebrity interviews with older performers as well as the more usual articles on health and beauty.

In addition to these titles, there is a huge market for women's weeklies. The traditional format, dominated by IPC's *Woman*, *Woman's Own*, and *Woman's Weekly*, concentrated on home and family. The entry of *Bella* (H. Bauer) and *Best* (Gruner & Jahr) into the UK market in the late 1980s brought a market shake-up with a stronger emphasis on gossip and chat, causing IPC to respond with the launch of *Chat*. Add to the mix celebrity news and entertainment, exemplified by *Hello!* (Hello Limited),

**Figure 1.5** *Glamour*, December 2005. Used with kind permission from James White/*Glamour* © The Condé Nast Publications Ltd.

*OK!* (Northern and Shell), and *Heat* (Emap) and the weekly market has become a hotly contested battleground.

As with the men's market, women's weekly titles are currently among the fastest growing publications in the UK (comprising sales of nearly 10 million each month in 2006), the bestsellers including *Pick Me Up* (IPC) and *Take a Break* (H. Bauer) with a focus on real-life stories.

## Men's magazines

As previously noted, for a long period it was felt that the market for general men's titles was moribund, the phrase 'men's magazines' being synonymous with soft core pornography. This was despite the fact that men had bought magazines such as *Weekend* and *Tit-Bits* in their hundreds of thousands, and for more than the inevitable pin-ups that accompanied them.

Men's monthlies have declined from their high point in the late 1990s, with some titles such as *Arena* (Emap) and *Loaded* (IPC) having suffered more than others. While attracting a smaller overall readership than general women's titles, however, it still remains an attractive market for advertisers and *FHM* (Emap) remains a substantial seller on the newsstands, although the US edition closed in 2006 and in the UK sales dropped from a highpoint of half a million to around 300,000 in 2007. Other monthlies include *Esquire* (National Magazines), and *GQ* (Condé Nast) at one end, which see themselves as somewhat more elegant than competitors such as *Maxim* (Dennis) and *Front* (SMD).

Recently, however, the men's market has seen most activity in weekly publications. As *Take a Break* achieves sales of around 1.2 million a month, Emap and IPC aggressively sought to create an equally lucrative audience among men, launching *Zoo* and *Nuts*, respectively, in January 2004. Both titles concentrated on models (often topless), football and light-hearted features or reviews, and achieved significant sales in the first few weeks (between 200,000 and 300,000 copies), although these figures dropped with subsequent price rises.

## Teen magazines

Unlike both men's and women's general titles, teen magazines did not really exist before 1960 when *Honey* was launched by Fleetway, very much a reaction to the 'invention' of the teenager in the 1950s.

Teen magazines are almost entirely a female phenomenon, the main alternative for males of the same age being comics. This is also a market that has seen considerable flux, with titles launching and closing very quickly. Compared to adult sectors, which measure the age of their core demographic in decades, the market for a particular teenage title is extremely narrow and will only appeal to a reader for a couple of years.

In 2006, the main titles were *Sugar* (HFUK), *Bliss* (Emap), *Cosmo Girl* (National Magazines), *Shout* (DC Thomson) and *Mizz* (Panini), with some long-standing magazines such as *19* (IPC) and *J-17* (previously *Just 17*, Emap) having closed in the previous years. The remaining magazines, however, can still expect sales of between 100,000 and 200,000 each month.

During the past two decades, various titles in this sector have aroused concern among parents, politicians and other adult readers outside their target audience because of a focus on sexuality – not just in terms of content but also the style of representation (particularly after *Loaded* transformed consumer magazines in 1994). Publishers have responded that they are often reacting to more general trends among teenagers, who wanted to purchase older titles and migrated to older celebrity and general women's titles at an earlier age.

More recently there has been a tendency to emphasise how these magazines may help teenagers deal with problems, and the PPA established the Teen Magazine Arbitration Panel (TMAP), a self-regulatory body which, among other things, tries to ensure titles present sexual content in an appropriate manner.

## B2B

While the largest circulating titles are aimed at general consumers, by far the largest number of publications consists of magazines aimed at specific professions, with more than 5,000 titles in the UK according to the PPA. The business-to-business (B2B) sector, which used to be known as trade magazines, largely consists of controlled circulation titles that are distributed directly to individuals and companies working in particular industries, although some are also sold on the newsstand. Examples include *Farmers Weekly* (Reed Business Information), *The Architects' Journal* (Emap) and *Press Gazette* (Wilmington Media Ltd).

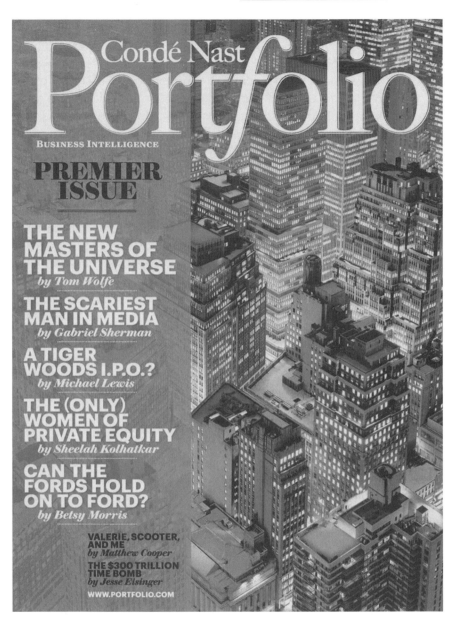

**Figure 1.6** *Condé Nast Portfolio*

While a substantial number of B2B titles are glossies that (in format if not content) look rather similar to consumer magazines, many also appear more like newspapers and some take the form of newsletters. As well as demonstrating more diversity than the consumer sector in terms of the type of publications, the B2B market also tends to provide a great many other services to the businesses it serves. These include directories, web sites and conferences, with ABC and BPA auditing electronic versions of magazines such as web pages and PDF files that can be sent out via email. As such, business and professional magazines are merely part of a communications sector that is estimated to be worth £13.7 billion.

Currently, ABC audits approximately 800 B2B magazines, and obviously the differences in terms of circulation between these titles and the bestselling consumer magazines are dramatic. While the top-selling consumer title is bought by nearly 1.5 million people (*What's On TV*), the biggest circulating business magazine in the period from July 2005 to June 2006 was the *RCN Bulletin*, reaching nearly 374,000 nursing professionals.

The big difference, of course, is that the audience for such titles is much more tightly focused and, as such, publishers can charge much more per capita for advertising. For example, a popular general women's magazine such as *Cosmopolitan* can expect to charge between £17,000 to £27,000 per page of advertising depending on position if it has a readership of half a million in the UK. By contrast, a specialist magazine for the aeronautics industry, *Flight International*, charges nearly £8,000 yet only has a worldwide circulation of approximately 42,000; the difference is that those readers include the chief executives of airlines and senior military staff who will be responsible for huge budgets.

The relationship with advertising in the B2B sector can be a difficult one because so many titles rely entirely on ads for revenue. At the same time, and this is particularly true for the top-circulating titles that are ABC audited, the relationship with a professional readership requires a degree of trust and, indeed, the best B2B titles are often better in terms of their journalistic standards than a great many consumer magazines.

Staff working on business publications build up a degree of expertise in their field, and so often produce news stories and features that are comparable to the best newspaper publishing in the UK. Unfortunately, there are also plenty of trade titles that offer reviews that are little more than puff pieces for advertisers.

Because of the sheer diversity of the B2B sector, this book cannot hope to give a comprehensive guide to the market, but will offer a sample of three broad sectors.

## Management and professional

Many large circulating B2B titles are general management publications such as *Business Network* (NFSE Sales) and *Financial Management* (Caspian Publishing) that are aimed across a wide range of businesses, offering news and advice to those responsible for running and administrating companies in the UK. Other magazines concentrate much more on specific professions including accountancy (*Accounting and Business*, ACCA), the legal profession (*Law Society's Gazette*, Council of the Law Society), and education (*Education Week*, Editorial Projects in Education).

While the majority of B2B publications will be released by commercial publishers, it is worth noting that a significant number of controlled circulation titles are also published and distributed by the professional bodies responsible for setting standards.

## Trade and industry

While professional titles tend to target a particular type of individual working in an organisation, there are also wider trade titles that provide an overview of an industry, including the motor trade (*Auto Service and Repair*, McMillan-Scott), agriculture (*Farmer's Guardian*, CMP Information Ltd), the grocery trade (*The Grocer*, William Reed), and computing (*Manufacturing Computer Solutions*, Findlay Publications).

## Medical

Medical titles are, of course, professional and/or trade titles, the same as any other business publication. The reason for considering them separately is to demonstrate the significance of the NHS as one of the largest employers in Europe, which, in turn, generates a huge market for information at a range of levels. Thus titles dealing with medicine include those aimed at doctors and consultants (GMC *Today*, The General

Medical Council), nurses (*RCN Bulletin*) and pharmaceutical publications (*The Pharmaceutical Journal*, Royal Pharmaceutical Society). GMC *Today* and the *RCN Bulletin* are the top-circulating B2B titles in the UK with a significant lead over other magazines.

## Contract publishing

The highest circulating magazines in the UK are not those bought on the newsstand by general consumers, but titles produced for companies such as Sky, the Automobile Association and the main supermarkets. In 2006, the title with the largest distribution was *Sky The Magazine* (with more than 7 million subscriptions), followed by magazines for Asda, Tesco and the National Trust. Contract publishing (or custom publishing as it is also referred to) is a relatively new phenomenon in the UK, having only really taken hold when Redwood Publishing started business in the mid-1980s.

Most custom magazines are given away free, although a few are also sold on the newsstand, such as the dieting magazine *LighterLife* (Square One) and the TV tie-in *Location, Location, Location* (Brooklands). Contract publishing agencies produce magazines, marketing materials, and newsletters for corporations to be read by their customers or employees.

A feature that the larger custom titles share with other commercial publications is a tendency towards internationalisation. At the same time, these titles tend to be much more specialised than mainstream magazines, so that different versions will be tailored to different types of reader. Another distinction from general magazine publishing is that often the companies involved in contract publishing are also engaged in advertising, so that the relationship between editorial and advertising is much closer.

The largest contract publisher in the UK is John Brown Citrus Publishing (formed in 2002 by a merger between John Brown Publishing, previously responsible for *Viz* as well as a number of other consumer titles, and Citrus), with clients that include Waitrose and Virgin Atlantic. The company that revolutionised contract publishing, Redwood Publishing, was briefly controlled by BBC magazines before coming under the control of the advertising agency Abbot Mead Vickers. It is very active internationally, for example, also being involved in selling advertising in the US.

## Partwork publishing

A rather specialist sector, particularly as the market is dominated by one publisher. A partwork is a series of magazines designed to be bound together as a complete book, usually accompanied by a free gift. Although the format is generally similar for such magazines (no advertising, building up information on a particular individual, group or extending information from simple to more complex subjects), the types of titles published are extremely varied and cover subjects such as computers, DIY, art, history and children's books.

The most important publisher, responsible for the majority of such titles in Europe and other parts of the globe as well as the UK, is De Agostini. An Italian company founded in 1901, it published its first partwork in 1959 (an Italian encyclopaedia). At any one time it will be publishing some 20 to 30 partwork magazines, each of which will appear in a limited number of issues before being completed.

## News supplements

Newspaper magazines are distributed on Saturday and Sunday with the main UK newspapers, something that started in 1962 with the launch of the *Sunday Times Magazine*. Many of these are general interest supplements, combining some element of current affairs or reportage alongside leisure, sport, home, health and fashion articles, but an increasing number of titles also produce specialist magazines for sport or food. Indeed, while the glossy magazines tend to stand out from the rest of a newspaper, the tendency for the dailies and Sunday editions to be divided into sections for sport, reviews, technology, motoring and so on has led to what is commonly referred to as the 'magazinification' of newspapers.

As the circulations for the magazines as part of newspaper distributions are huge (nearly 3.27 million for *Sunday*, sold with *News of the World*, and over 2.3 million for *The Mail on Sunday*'s *YOU* magazine), these titles have an extremely significant readership base in the UK, attracting considerable advertising revenue and also being able to dedicate resources to developing new markets, such as *The Observer*'s monthly sports and food magazines, launched in 2001.

## Main publishers

**H. Bauer:** Established in Hamburg in 1875, H. Bauer Publishing claims to be the largest privately owned publisher in Europe, publishing 120 magazines in 13 countries. Its entry into the UK market was marked by the publication of *Bella* in 1987, with an emphasis on real-life stories, and again attracted attention in 1990 with the launch of *Take a Break*, with sales of over a million a week. It plays a major role in the women's and TV guide markets, making it one of the top three consumer publishers in the UK in terms of retail sales.

**BBC Magazines:** Part of the BBC's commercial services, BBC Magazines produces titles that are often (although not exclusively) linked to television programming for which it generates further revenue. The company concentrated on producing *Radio Times* and the *Listener* from the 1920s until the 1980s when it licensed the *Clothes Show* title and then extended its portfolio, primarily because of increased competition from TV listings magazines. It bought the company Redwood (which it later sold), and is now responsible for many top-selling consumer titles in the UK, including *Top Gear*, *Gardener's World* and *Focus* (the last of the magazines it retained from a group of Origin titles, bought in 2004, the rest of which were sold off in 2006).

**Condé Nast:** A US-based publisher that specialises in upmarket publications and operates throughout Europe, the company was founded in 1909 when Condé Montrose Nast took over *Vogue*. The parent company is responsible for 18 publications, including *The New Yorker*, *GQ*, *Glamour* and *Condé Nast Traveller*.

**Dennis Publishing:** The largest UK independent publishing company (and often one of the most idiosyncratic due to the guiding principles of its founder, Felix Dennis, who was prosecuted in 1971 as co-editor of *Oz*), Dennis Publishing was founded in 1973 and gained an early success with *Kung-Fu Magazine*. In the late 1980s, *Computer Shopper* was the largest selling consumer IT title, while the 1990s saw the launch of *Maxim*, one of the highest circulating men's magazines in both the UK and the US. It largely targets male readers, with other publications including *PC Pro*, *Poker Player* and the car magazine *Evo*.

**Emap:** After IPC/Time Warner, the second-largest consumer publisher in the UK and the largest trade exhibition organiser, having started out as a regional newspaper company in 1947. B2B publishing is grouped in the Emap Communications division, currently in the process of being sold to Guardian Media Group, with consumer titles taken care of by the appropriately named Emap Consumer Media division; the company has a large number of subsidiaries in the UK, however, including Emap Elan, being bought out by H. Bauer at the time of writing, operating across a large number of multimedia platforms (and being a forerunner of cross-media advertising). While consolidating its hold on the UK market, it has changed strategy internationally, having withdrawn from the US. Key brands include *FHM*, *Heat* and *Retail Week*.

**Future:** One of the largest magazine publishers in the UK, Future began in 1985 by producing computer magazines before expanding into other hobby and leisure interests. It was briefly owned by Pearson but later began a rapid process of expansion in 2004 (which was cut back in 2006). The company concentrates on niche markets such as general computer and gaming magazines, entertainment, sport and music, with titles such as *Edge*, *Total Film* and *T3*.

**Hachette Filipacchi UK:** The UK subsidiary of Hachette Filipacchi Medias, itself a subsidiary of Legardère Media, one of the world's largest magazine publishers (and which began in Paris as a book publisher in 1826). Hachette took over Attic Futura in 2002; previously the company had worked with Emap to produce titles such as *Elle*. Although the parent company has 245 titles, more than half of its sales come from outside France. Its other magazines include *Sugar* and *Red*.

**Haymarket:** Founded in 1957 as Cornmarket Press by Clive Labovitch and Michael Heseltine, the company became Haymarket in 1964 following investment by the printer Hazell Watson & Viney. Haymarket produces a number of popular consumer and B2B titles, as well as several shows for the BBC such as *BBC Gardener's World Live*. It moved into the profitable medical market in the 1970s, and among its brands are *Autocar*, *MediaWeek* and *Stuff*.

**IPC Media:** The largest consumer publisher in the UK, and part of the Time Warner group since 2001, the International Publishing Corporation was formed in 1963 from three magazine groups with roots extending back to the launch of *The Field* in 1853. It publishes 80 magazines across a diverse range, with separate divisions such as IPC Connect which produces women's weeklies, and IPC Ignite which targets men's lifestyle and entertainment. Its publications include *Nuts*, *Woman's Weekly* and *TV Times*.

**National Magazine Company:** Part of Hearst Corporation, the American company established in 1910 that is one of the largest magazine companies in the world (with international editions of its titles in over 100 countries) and is also a major US newspaper publisher and broadcaster. It took over the UK publications of Gruner & Jahr in 2000 and produces some of the most high-profile consumer titles in the country, including *Cosmopolitan*, *Esquire* and *She*.

**Northern & Shell:** Established in 1974, Northern & Shell made its fortunes in pornographic magazines before moving into the mainstream market in the 1980s and then newspaper publishing. Its most successful title is *OK!* and it also publishes *New!* and *Star*.

**Reader's Digest:** One of the world's most successful publications, the American edition was first published in 1922 to offer condensed versions of articles from popular magazines and was launched in the UK in 1938. The company also produces a number of books.

**Reed Business Publishing:** A subsidiary of Reed Elsevier, a leading global publisher formed from the merger of Reed International (established 1894) and Elsevier NV (1880) in 1993, the company concentrates on medical, legal, education and business titles, with magazines such as *Flight International*, *Farmers Weekly* and *New Scientist*.

## The role of the Periodical Publishers Association (PPA)

The Periodical Publishers Association (PPA, www.ppa.co.uk) is the body responsible for magazine and professional media publishers in the UK, promoting and protecting the interests of the industry in general and its members (almost 400 companies) in particular. The PPA is itself a member of UK Publishing Media (www.publishingmedia.org.uk), an alliance of newspaper, magazine, book and data publishers that covers an industry worth £22 billion (double the pharmaceutical industry) and employs more than 16,000 people.

The precursor of the PPA, the Society of Weekly Newspaper and Periodical Proprietors, was founded in 1913 under the chairmanship of Sir George Allardice Riddell. This, in turn, split into the Periodical, Trade Press and Weekly Newspaper Proprietors Association and The Newspaper Proprietors' Association in 1941, although the combination of weekly newspapers and periodicals was short lived, leading to a separate Periodical Trade Press (PTP) association in 1942. By 1967, The Periodical Proprietors Association had become the Periodical Publishers Association.

The aim of the PPA, as well as to act on behalf of the majority of companies in the UK, is to maintain professional publishing standards and, where possible, raise standards to ensure a healthy industry. It achieves this in a number of ways: first, by running conferences, training courses and awards ceremonies to recognise best practice; second, by providing information via its web site and publications on issues such as legal matters and publishing procedures; and third, via the Periodicals Training Council (PTC), which works both with academic institutions to accredit courses and with publishing companies to provide specific training requirements.

As well as representing members that publish over 2,260 consumer and business titles, responsible for some 80 per cent of the UK market by turnover if not quantity of titles, these companies also produce directories and web sites, conferences, exhibitions and awards, as well as often having ties to broadcast media. Full membership includes magazine publishers such as Emap, IPC and BBC magazines, while associate membership recognises suppliers to the industry, such as design bureaus, distribution services and paper manufacturers.

## The PPA Code of Publishing Practice

Members of the PPA are encouraged to engage in best practice as part of upholding professional standards, including participating in ABC auditing to ensure that circulation figures are independently verified, and participating in self-regulatory arrangements.

In particular, the PPA code covers the following, whereby members agree to:

- Observe the British Code of Advertising, Sales Promotion and Direct Marketing Practice and contribute to funding arrangements through the Advertising Standards Board of Finance (ASBOF).

- Abide by the Press Code of Practice, accept and act upon the Press Complaints Commission findings and register with and contribute to the funding of the Press Board of Finance (PressBOF).
- Abide by the terms of the PPA Mail Order Protection Scheme.
- Agree to take account of PPA guidelines for best practices for list owners, telephone selling, the operation of Royal Mail Presstream, special advertising opportunities, the coverage of sexual subject matter in teenage magazines, online publishing, editorial content and other areas for which the PPA Board issues recommendations.

## A career in magazines

While choosing the appropriate degree (undergraduate or postgraduate) is increasingly the most important step in getting started on a career in magazines, it is not the only factor that the aspiring journalist should consider. Work experience, as with so many sectors of the media, is often crucial.

Because of the specialised and fragmentary nature of magazine publishing, the first thing to consider is your own interests, what your pastimes and hobbies are. Many graduates, at least in the early stages of study, tend to gravitate towards general men's and women's magazines, or general interest titles and supplements, but competition for these titles can be extremely severe. Working out where you will be able to engage your own interests with a more specialist consumer or B2B title is frequently a much better strategy for getting a work placement.

When applying with a CV, the Periodicals Training Council (PTC) makes several useful recommendations, most notably that the variety of publications within the magazine industry make identikit applications extremely unhelpful. As such, the initial approach should indicate that you have undertaken some research into your target publication and market. At the very least, you should find the appropriate editor's name (consult the contact section of a title, as well as BRAD or *The Writers' and Artists' Yearbook*), but also where you will be able to fit your talents to a particular organisation – perhaps because an editor is due to go on holiday.

The PTC also observes that the ideal candidate would write like an angel, have a solid news- and features-based qualification, and an interest in the magazine topic since an early age, although in practice two out of three will lead to an interview. For further information to help you get started on a career in magazines, consult the PTC careers guide, *Your Future in Magazines*, which covers publishing, sales, production and marketing as well as editorial and writing.

## 2

# The business of magazines

This chapter will consider the structures of a 'typical' magazine company, by which is meant a commercial organisation whose main business is magazine production, whether consumer or B2B. However, this is by no means the only type of organisation involved in creating magazines: charities, religious groups, colleges and universities, businesses – all sorts of groups and individuals – may produce in-house or small-circulation titles. In addition, someone reading this book will presumably have a strong interest in producing their own title, perhaps for personal interest, but without necessarily being tied to a commercial publisher.

Indeed, even if attention is restricted to commercial magazine companies, the notion that there is a clear conventional structure runs into various difficulties. Some magazines are large operations with huge circulations and staffing levels to match, comprising a small to medium business in their own right; other titles, although happily turning a profit, may consist of a small team sharing responsibilities for editorial and design that would be divided more clearly in a larger company.

The largest enterprises, such as Emap, IPC and National Magazines, will have a managing director, president or chief executive officer, responsible ultimately for the business concerns and holdings of a media company as a whole. That particular role is far beyond the remit of this book: instead, the focus in this chapter will be on the role of the publisher and certain other related positions, such as advertising, marketing and administrative directors. The functions of a circulation director will be considered in the next chapter, while later sections will turn to the roles of the editor and art editor.

## The role of the publisher

Usually the most senior position on a magazine, the publisher is responsible for maintaining a magazine's viability in commercial terms, that is, by promoting its visibility in the marketplace and ensuring that sufficient revenues are generated to keep a title in operation. As the majority of magazines rely on advertising for profitability, so publishers tend to rise through the ranks of advertising sales, although some may come from editorial or circulation backgrounds. Although the largest media companies will have a higher level of executive management above the level of publisher, in some smaller companies a publisher may be responsible directly for several titles and even be the proprietor of the company.

The publisher, then, can be considered the general manager of a title, responsible for its growth and success and, as such, has to be a strategist who pays attention not only to the business of magazines, but also with a wider eye on the general economy and conditions in the market. He or she will need to be aware of the types of audiences that are attractive to advertisers, as well as what readers are looking for from particular magazine markets (although this is much more of a concern for the editor).

Above all, the publisher needs to have a clear understanding of the 'mission' of a magazine, its purpose and aims: ideally these are determined in conjunction with the editor and, in a company that produces a number of titles, will also need to be determined in line with a corporate overview of the publishing company's aims. However, in such circumstances, the publisher also needs to be the champion of the magazine: in a drive to increase profitability, corporate management may frequently impose burdens on, or make changes to the mission of, a magazine that can generate revenues in the short term but are detrimental in the long term.

That said, however, a publisher always has to be interested in profit: without it, the vast majority of publications simply cease to exist, and while some journalists like to maintain a rather snooty attitude towards what they see as the filthy lucre of publishing, following a higher calling than mere advertising sales, there are very few journalists who are happy to pursue such a career without payment over the long term.

What is more, a publisher will also consider new ways to extend revenues taking the magazine as a core brand: a B2B publisher, for example, will probably look for opportunities to host conventions or trade shows related to their magazine mission. Some common ways of generating additional revenue include reprints or books, custom publishing for advertisers or other clients, market research, and buyers' guides and catalogues, as well as conferences and seminars.

## The publisher and management

In addition to the strategic role in developing a magazine, the publisher is also often involved in departmental management – although how much he or she actually participates in day-to-day decisions and operations will vary depending on the size of a particular title. In smaller, one-title set-ups, the publisher will take a more direct approach to managing such things as circulation and marketing, as well as the general running of the office, but for larger companies he or she will delegate knowledgeable and experienced personnel to run different sections. In all cases, however, senior managers such as editors, circulation and advertising directors will report to the publisher.

At the opposite end of the scale to single-title publications are multiple-title organisations where functions may be centralised. This makes sense for a number of day-to-day tasks, such as human resources and accounting or financial planning, which will require similar procedures from one title to the next. Advertising and editorial are rarely centralised, although certain elements of production such as liaison with printers will benefit from being run out of a single location. The downside of centralisation can be that a publisher feels a lack of control (or responsibility) for areas outside his or her direct management.

## Publishers and editorial

For a magazine to run successfully, the publisher will need to have an understanding of the ways in which different departments operate as a business. As has already been remarked, editorial and circulation will be dealt with in more detail elsewhere in this book, but it is worth bearing in mind how a publisher will typically organise the commercial running of his or her magazine.

In the vast majority of magazines other than those very few which are principally read as advertising catalogues, or promotional titles for 'hot' new products, editorial pages are key to commercial success. Consumers purchase titles to read features, reviews and news, and while the role of advertising should not be underestimated (in that a great deal of information other than simple consumer decisions can be gleaned from adverts), material produced by journalists and designers will be essential to making or breaking a magazine.

For the publisher, then, editorial is a major cost centre but an essential one: certainly for the editor it must seem that all other aspects of publishing are ultimately geared towards ensuring the continued growth and success of the content he or she is responsible for.

## Conflicts and agreement

While some publishers like to have a more hands-on approach to editorial, it is a rare magazine where this produces harmonious results. The setting up of a separate editorial fiefdom, however, is unlikely to be efficient. The publisher's role, then, is not to manage the writing, photography, layout and design of a magazine, but more to ensure that editorial principles are in line with the overall intentions and functions of a title and publishing company.

Publisher and editor should be in agreement as to the aims and intentions of the magazine, and very often in larger companies the publisher serves as a buffer between corporate management and the editor and also, often, in the tricky relationship between editorial and advertising. Frequently, publishing houses will have policies in place to ensure that there is a proper procedure for maintaining relations between editorial and sales, the latter notoriously interested in influencing what appears in the former, as good reviews or product placements can make their job much easier although being seen as a soft touch for advertisers can be detrimental to the long-term interests of a magazine. In some cases, there may even be a policy of separation between those departments.

Although publishers are unlikely to have come from a writing background, their knowledge of the market should make them good readers and there are plenty of publishers who are avid consumers of competitor titles. This, in turn, can make them an important sounding board for editorial decisions. The publisher will also have an essential role to play in legal issues that may arise from editorial, having responsibilities with the editor concerning libel, for example. Finally, an editor will have to discuss and arrange budgets in conjunction with the publisher.

## Advertising and media sales

For the vast majority of magazines, advertising is the key to financial success and, therefore, is an area that deeply involves publishers, so much so that the publisher is also sometimes the advertising director on smaller magazines. Certainly a key role for any publisher is to help build relations with the most important advertising clients, and to ensure that a title provides a suitable environment which will be appealing to them.

For example, just about every market has important advertisers who are also competitors, and if a title is seen to give preferential treatment to one over another this can generate negative reactions: one area that can be extremely significant in this regard is when placing adverts on prime spots in a title, such as the inside front or back covers, or nearer the front of a magazine. Because of this, publishers have to put in place a clear policy that will explain why such decisions are made.

In addition, a good publisher will want to be seen as an important figure in the industry of which his or her magazine is a part. Liaising with clients (who may also be advertisers) involves attending conferences, trade shows and any other important event where the profile of a title can be raised, and to which he or she can make a contribution in terms of expertise and knowledge.

Over a little more than a hundred years, magazines have become extremely successful vehicles for advertising, but they are just one platform that is available to advertisers. When selling space in a magazine, the advertising director along with the publisher must consider what alternatives may be open, such as television as well as other competing titles, and the purpose of a campaign.

Advertisers will have a particular audience that they wish to reach, and sometimes a campaign will be seasonal, such as in the run-up to Christmas. Sales teams will wish to consider the strategy for when they approach advertisers as well as the reasons why their title will be more appealing.

## Advertisers, agencies and sales teams

The advertising director will have a responsibility to research the market, to know companies and their products in order to discover which are more suitable than others. A consumer IT title, for example, will bring little benefit to manufacturers or service providers who are mainly responsible for supplying large companies.

Market segmentation is often extremely important: some advertisers divide potential consumers along demographic lines such as age or income, while others see occupational categories as more important. Of course, the success of previous advertising campaigns (particularly ones which drew positive responses from the publisher's own title) needs to be kept in mind.

Nearly all advertising – certainly large-scale campaigns by national or international companies – are run through advertising agencies, and it is usually these that a sales team will be dealing with. Approaching a producer directly can be counter-productive, not merely because a company will have hired such an agency to provide expertise, but because this can be seen to be going behind the agency's back: fairly understandably, they will not be inclined to place any of their other clients in a title that engages in what they see as sharp practice.

One other factor facing magazine publishers is whether to have an in-house media sales team or to use a third-party sales agency. An in-house team has the advantage of knowing the magazine in much more detail and providing full control to the publisher, but has the disadvantage of higher costs and requiring greater management.

Using an agency can provide a possible existing customer base for new publications, and is a resource that can be used as and when required – but is also unlikely ever to know as much about the magazine as a media sales team that can be trained and build up experience over time. Where centralisation does tend to occur, it is often in large publishing companies that offer media sales over their own stable of titles.

## Advertising departments

How large an advertising department is depends on the number of pages of advertising that are sold and the volume of advertising revenue. Most titles cannot survive on circulation revenues alone – and for controlled circulation magazines that do not charge a cover price their income is usually entirely dependent on media sales.

In the UK, as opposed to the US, it is unusual for a sales director to also have regional directors, but he or she will often be responsible for a number of account managers, each of whom has responsibility for particular clients or areas of media sales within a magazine. In the very smallest titles, the sales director may even be the publisher working with one or two sales staff.

The advertising manager or director will be responsible for providing estimates of revenue as well as devising a sales strategy (in conjunction with the publisher), part of which will involve developing relations with advertisers and their agencies. Providing realistic estimates is important because it will determine the level of spending throughout all levels of a magazine and so, of course, influence a title's profit or loss.

Part of the sales strategy includes taking into account short-term economic conditions, but also paying attention to the market in which a brand operates. In doing this, the sales manager will need to understand why current advertisers buy space in the title for which he or she works, and why similar advertisers do not – and what can be done to bring them on board.

While some titles maintain a more or less strict division between sales and editorial, to work out this strategy effectively requires cooperation between him or her and the editor. Finally, he or she will also have responsibilities for the sales team (including hiring and firing) and for the department budget.

## Media sales

Someone working in media sales will be given responsibility for a number of accounts, involving establishing and maintaining relationships with clients and their agencies, representing the magazine and closing sales. A main task of an account manager is to make sales calls, either to set up initial meetings or follow up, all of which build the rapport between an advertiser or potential advertiser and the magazine.

While email and other forms of electronic communication have become much more important in recent years, the phone and face-to-face meetings remain the main ways to sell space. The task for someone working in sales is to get to see an advertiser in what will often be a busy schedule: such meetings are often accompanied by a formal or informal presentation in which a pitch will be made explaining what the benefits are for an advertiser to buy space in the magazine.

Account managers will also often have to send through technical or legal material (such as page sizes for adverts, schedules and contracts), and nearly every medium- to large-scale title will run some form of customer relationship management (CRM) system, a database in which contact details and information on sales are stored, and which members of a team are meant to update on a regular basis.

Once he or she has made contact with a client and their agency, a sales representative must maintain regular contact, and an important role is played by entertainment, such as lunch or evening events: for dedicated sales people in the media business, this is rarely a 9 to 5 job. As well as building up knowledge of the brand itself, such a person must also learn about the needs of a client. Members of a sales team will be expected to communicate news about the magazine in a useful way and get to know different people working in clients' markets.

As with many such jobs, media sales can bring a considerable amount of stress and the churn rate of hiring and firing can be fairly high (certainly much higher than editorial). Payment packages are almost invariably in the form of a basic salary plus bonuses for what are called OTE (over target earnings): if your allotted space to sell is ten pages each month, and you meet that target, then you will receive your basic salary, but increasing that amount can improve earnings significantly.

## Ad placement

Agencies can place advertisements in a magazine in a variety of ways. The most common form is display advertising, usually a single page or double-page spread (DPS), although there are plenty of titles that offer display advertising that can take up a fraction of a page such as a half or quarter and some that will offer a gatefold, a page that folds out. This is usually glossy and full colour, although some magazines will offer full page black and white ads if they do not print throughout in colour.

The second most common format is classified, which, as with newspapers, can range from a few lines costing a few pounds to more usual boxouts with small images and contact information, or even occasionally full-page ads. While classified advertising is typically much cheaper than display ads, for some brands this can be a very profitable enterprise: charging tens or hundreds of pounds can make a single page of space more lucrative than a single page of display advertising.

For some markets, such as those that rely on recruitment media sales, classified advertising is extremely important. In addition, businesses may print their own brochures or other material which is then bound into the magazine or distributed as loose inserts.

Where advertisements are placed in a magazine can have a major impact on how they are received by the reader. It is for this reason that many (though not all) titles charge more depending on where an advert appears. To appear on the back or inside covers, for example, is a premium position that will cost most, while many titles charge more for ads placed near the front third or quarter than for those appearing near the back. In addition to placement, publishers will often try to 'lock in' an advertiser for as long as possible, and the easiest way to do this is to offer a discount for ads that are taken out over more than one issue.

## Rate cards

Because costs can vary according to position, important information that publishers offer to prospective advertisers as part of a media pack (covered in more detail in the next chapter) is in the form of a rate card. This will list information such as the cost for full page and DPS advertising, as well as fractions of a page if offered, depending on position and factoring in such things as discounts for a series of ads over three, six or 12 months.

In addition, a magazine will be required to state the terms and conditions of the contract between it and an advertiser, such as the consequences of cancelling an advert, who is responsible for accuracy and payment. Also, the advertiser will have a strong interest in the number of copies a title sells, which will be considered under auditing in the next chapter.

Wherever possible, a publisher will try to move a title towards a rate card, a clear set of prices that he or she believes the market can afford.

## Advertising rates effective 1/1/2007

All prices are in UK Sterling; VAT will be added at applicable rate. Series discounts are available as listed below (approx 15% for a four-series, 30% for an eight-series).

All adverts are full colour, except entries in the Specialists' Directory, which may be either colour or mono.

| SPECIAL POSITIONS | Single entry | 4-series | 8-series |
| --- | --- | --- | --- |
| Inside front, DPS | 5560 | 4700 | 3910 |
| Inside front, full page | 3130 | 2650 | 2350 |
| Inside back cover | 3130 | 2650 | 2350 |
| Outside back cover | 3650 | 3100 | 2550 |

| AGAINST EDITORIAL | Single entry | 4-series | 8-series |
| --- | --- | --- | --- |
| DPS | 4710 | 4010 | 3535 |
| Full page | 2860 | 2430 | 2140 |
| Half page | 1630 | 1380 | 1220 |
| Quarter page | 980 | 835 | 695 |

| SPECIALISTS' DIRECTORY | Single entry | 4-series | 8-series |
| --- | --- | --- | --- |
| Eighth page colour | 555 | 475 | 410 |
| Eighth page mono | 475 | 400 | 315 |

### Additional Discounts Available
Registered Charity 20%
Approved Agency 10%

### Pre-payment discount
An *additional discount* can be applied to 4-series and 8-series rates for settlement in full for the series within 14 days of order, instead of the usual payment terms of within 30 days of publication. Prepayment of a 4-series attracts a *10%* discount, and for an 8-series *20%*. A single-entry booking attracts no discount.

**Figure 2.1** A typical advertising rate card from *Wanderlust*

Difficulty often occurs if a particular industry is going through troubled times: at such moments, publishers may lose money because advertisers tighten their belts and do not spend as much on ad campaigns.

The danger that can ensue when haggling over prices is that if an agency discovers that a competitor has preferential rates that are not transparent (that is, printed on the rate card), it may also seek to negotiate its own discounts and a magazine is soon caught in a vicious circle where all its advertisers seek to pay less than the going rate. During a downturn publishers may decide to lose advertising rather than cut their rate card, gambling that when the market improves clients will return at the full rate.

From the advertiser's point of view, one common way of measuring the effectiveness of an advert is to measure it against a cost per mil, or mille (CPM, also known as CPT, or cost per thousand) basis. This is the relative cost of reaching 1,000 readers for a particular advertisement.

## The effects of advertising and advertorial

The conventional and liberal view of the effects of advertising is that consumers are rational buyers who effectively know what is best for them. In relation to this, they make independent and informed choices and it is the task of the advertiser to ensure that they receive the most appropriate information to help them make that choice. This certainly is the opinion of organisations such as the Advertising Standards Agency, which sees its role as to ensure that they will not be misled by false advertising – and which can insist that such ads are removed and fines levied on those who create them.

Against this view is one that developed from post-Marxist cultural traditions, which points out that branding relies on fantasy and that compulsive buying indicates irrational reactions on the part of the consumer. In addition, following Bourdieu (1986), the notion that we are clearly thinking, rational consumers has to take into account such things as family socialisation and education, which determine the taste for a wide range of goods. What Bourdieu calls 'cultural capital' comes (among other things) from the ways in which we are judged according to our taste – and, in turn, we are what we buy.

For magazines, the relationship is rarely this vexed in terms of building a readership – successful editors realise that they depend on media sales for the continued existence of their titles (and their jobs), but problems can arise in terms of the role of maintaining editorial independence from advertisers.

The relationships developed in magazines are triangular, between the staff producing titles, their readers and the advertisers. The importance of magazines to the latter is that they deliver potential consumers who will buy their products, but to maintain a high circulation (and thus those potential consumers) depends on trust existing between editorial and the audience: if a magazine is seen to be straying too close to its advertisers, for example, by delivering reviews that are seen as not independent, it can too easily lose readers.

The ways in which this delicate relationship is sometimes developed can be seen by two attempts to reach readers via other means than direct advertising, such as 'advertorial' or sponsorship. Advertorial is usually indicated in a magazine or newspaper by a phrase such as 'advertising special feature', and is material produced by a company to promote their products that looks like a normal feature in the title in which it appears. It will typically be written by in-house staff (in consultation with the advertiser or its agency), and is justified usually on the grounds that it provides something 'extra' for the reader in terms of providing information.

The question remains, however, whether it is acceptable for ads to 'do' editorial: certainly, advertorial was rare in quality publications until the late 1990s, but has been gaining ground over the past decade or so. Advertisers are often keen to pay more for this type of promotion because they feel they can gain the credibility of the title, but although often extremely lucrative for a magazine it can also be damaging if pursued too far.

## Sponsorship

Sponsorship is another route taken to avoid direct advertising, and has long been accepted as part of the commercial background for most commercial magazines as well as other media. Sponsors (or editors) can emphasise the separation between magazine and advertiser by issuing a separate supplement, or indicate a closer relationship by running regularly sponsored pages, such as a letters or competition page. The phrase 'in relation with' usually indicates that the sponsor has some say in the final appearance of the page or product, while 'sponsored by' tends to mean that the advertiser simply wishes to gain prestige from an association with a brand, with content being editorially driven.

While the links between editorial and advertising can sometimes be strained, with the latter seeking to influence the former, there is one important area in which they must be developed if a title is to have any hope of being successful. The editor must keep constant links with the advertising team to let them know what features and stories will be appearing in future issues. With advance knowledge of the editorial calendar – which will be available to the entire magazine staff and, indeed, to external sources as well – the sales team can start to target potential contacts who may be willing to advertise in a particular issue that they know is covering subjects pertinent to their business.

## Marketing and promotion

Along with sales, another area that a publisher often has direct involvement with is marketing and promotion. Just as a title has to attract advertising investment to survive, so it also has to sell itself to make sure that it is as prominent as possible in the marketplace.

Larger magazines may have a dedicated marketing manager, or a marketing department that operates over several titles, but for smaller publications it may be that the publisher takes direct responsibility for promoting his or her title. Whoever is in charge, the task for marketing and promotion is to ensure that a definite brand is in the reader's mind when he or she goes out to buy a magazine.

In contrast to newspapers, where despite declining circulations (often a result of increasing cover prices) readers will often remain loyal to their particular national or local daily or weekly newspaper, rarely if ever buying the competition, magazine readers – at least for consumer titles – are notoriously promiscuous. Someone who buys *Nuts* one week might try out *Zoo* in another, or go for a monthly such as *FHM*.

In addition, certain types of magazines are seasonal in their sales: readers tend not to buy wedding titles every month of the year – or indeed, very often at all during their lives: in the months prior to a marriage, however, consumers may purchase a large number of competing titles for advice and tips in the run-up to the big day. What the marketing department will seek to do is ensure that, as much as possible, readers (and also advertisers) are aware of its title in the heavily competitive environment of the newsstand.

In addition to promoting the magazine, a marketing manager will often work in conjunction with the circulation department to find out what the readers want and think of a magazine, and in this respect can provide valuable information to the editorial department as well as the publisher. This may take the form of research via questionnaires within a title, phone polls or even focus groups, where ideas can be tested out with a smaller group of individuals.

Promotion can include advertising, for example, on television or billboards, to draw the public's attention to a new launch or changes that have been made to an old favourite: TV advertising is very rare for all but the largest general consumer titles, not merely because it is so expensive but also because most magazines have target markets that are very specific, and so will waste money appealing to a large television audience. For multi-title companies, advertising might also take place across related magazines owned by the same company. However, for titles with smaller revenues or with very focused audiences, such as controlled circulation B2B magazines, advertising might be dispensed with altogether. This does not mean, however, that other forms of promotion can be neglected.

## Promotional materials and public relations

One very common way of promoting a magazine to advertisers in particular is via media packs. These will be covered in more detail in the next chapter, but they are designed to help strengthen a magazine as a brand, positioning it in the market and indicating such things as the typical reader and audience, as well as providing useful information on advertising rates and technical information (such as page sizes) for advertisers providing electronic files.

Although television advertising can be seen as a waste of money, point of sale materials, while expensive, can be extremely useful in attracting the consumer's attention at the newsstand. These can include display cases that make a title stand out from the competition, and for which a newsagent will charge a premium, to cover mounts offering 'free' gifts to the reader.

While advertisers will often approach magazines requesting information such as media packs (or, increasingly, use the web), publishers will also maintain promotion lists for direct mailing. Similar lists will be used to target readers, but the big challenge lies in making such promotional materials interesting enough to appeal to an audience, whether attracting new readers to a magazine or sparking interest in advertising, that the promotional materials will not be discarded immediately as junk mail. To this end, a common tactic when appealing to readers is to link promotional materials to competitions which may or may not come through sponsorship.

A main point of liaison between a marketing manager and the editorial team comes from writing press releases. The purpose of such releases is to try to get stories and features covered in a title into the local or national press, radio or television. During the planning stage, an effective editor will alert the marketing department as to any potentially interesting stories, and they or one of their team may even be involved in the writing of press releases that are sent out.

Likewise, a marketing team will look for opportunities to promote a title by getting members of staff to appear in the media when a story breaks on which they can offer an authoritative perspective. This is something that is particularly important to the B2B market, where the role of experienced journalists as pundits helps improve the prestige of the magazine – as well as providing expert information for news and feature stories.

## The role of PR

PR plays an important role in magazines – usually because editors and journalists are on the receiving end of information and events provided by public relations companies. However, because a magazine's standing is important within the industry, many titles use PR techniques themselves to improve their relationships with advertisers and customers.

New titles will wish to create a buzz and spread the word that this is a magazine worth watching, while older brands will want to reiterate that they are market leaders in the field. To this end, as well as sending out press releases a marketing department may organise parties for such things as anniversaries or new launches, as well as sponsor events related to the magazine's core business.

When useful (or favourable) articles appear in a magazine, it is not unusual for advertisers to seek to use these in their own promotions, and so a marketing manager and publisher should have a policy on reprints, determining when and where copyrighted material from the title can appear and how much it costs to re-use in this way. For the advertiser, having won plaudits from a respectable title can be a way of improving its own standing, but sometimes companies may approach a magazine seeking to use information that is not directly related to one of their goods but offers information that they see as being useful to their customers.

Related to this is the potential for market research. A marketing department may often seek to generate information for its own uses by contacting readers and will also build up industry expertise through its editorial staff. As has already been noted when discussing different market sectors, B2B titles will often be involved in additional activities such as conferences and trade shows, and these can often be integral to the success of a title.

Such research can, for many titles of a specialist nature, move beyond simple promotion of the magazine and become the development of an industry, writing white papers for companies, for example, that bring together the fruits of research by various bodies.

## Administration

Of the remaining departments that the publisher has ultimate respon-sibility for, the duties of a circulation manager and the principles of distributing a title are the subject of the next chapter. One area that he or she has to consider, however, is the general office management for the title, including maintaining a reception and communications facilities for visitors to the title or others who may wish to get in touch, organising meetings between various departments within a magazine and also external bodies, such as insurers, legal firms or accountants.

## The magazine budget

The largest costs for a publisher are staff salaries and add-on costs (such as pension contributions) and production, including printing, paper and binding. Desktop publishing has brought down some costs by making it possible to take control of functions such as layout and design that were once undertaken by third parties, and advances in pre-press preparation such as the ability to print to plate have also brought savings, but at the same time a magazine has to invest in hardware and software in-house.

Paper and printing remain major costs and the relationship between a publisher and its printer is extremely important. For large titles with high-volume distributions, changing printers is not something undertaken lightly. Likewise, paper costs have to be constantly monitored.

Underlying these and other such activities is the financial management of a title, for which the publisher is responsible. If this is a single title, the publisher may also be the owner and so the financial health of his or her title can be a more personal concern; but even someone employed by a company will have a strong interest in the debt, cash and capital of the brand.

As well as profit or loss, they will have to pay attention to cash-flows and investors; as well as changes 'internal' to the magazine that may affect profitability, such as declining circulation or advertising, the publisher will need to pay attention to 'external' factors that could lead to an economic downturn and so affect a publisher as well as other sectors of the economy. If the year ahead looks poor, then budgets need to be arranged accordingly, otherwise there will be a potential disaster later on if revenues fall below budget and redundancies have to be made.

When preparing the budget for a magazine, whether a new title or ongoing financial planning, the publisher needs to take into account the following factors:

- The number of advertising pages, including display and classified, which will give an estimate of ad revenues for the year compared to the proposed rate card.
- Circulation estimates: on paid-for magazines, this will provide additional revenues from newsstand sales and subscriptions.
- Total number of editorial pages as well as advertising pages. An increase in both editorial and advertising will, of course, bring with it greater printing and production costs, although an increase in advertising pages also increases revenue.
- The print run, that is, how many copies of the magazine will be printed. This can provide a basic estimate of mechanical costs for printing, binding and distribution.
- The editorial/advertising (ed/ad) ratio, that is, the percentage of editorial pages printed against advertising ones. A magazine will have a target ratio, such as 70 per cent of editorial to 30 per cent of advertising: too much editorial will increase costs, but too little will make the title less appealing to readers.
- Staffing costs, including direct costs such as salaries and benefits, and other costs such as expenses.
- Other administrative and business overheads, such as insurance, rent, depreciation and repairs and maintenance.

With these figures, it is possible to work out a profit and loss record – how much the magazine needs to earn to break even or go into profit.

At the same time, while the budget tends to be set annually, the financial status of the magazine has to be monitored on a regular basis. So sales and circulation figures have to be compared to projections made in the annual budget to see whether revisions have to be made for the rest of the year.

Obviously, in most instances publishers are looking for any warning signs that they might not be hitting targets, but occasionally a lucky publisher may find themselves in a position where they go over target – which can bring its own problems: the proprietors of a magazine, when the market is in a good economic position, will expect growth year on year. If for some reason a title is particularly successful in one year, this may raise unrealistic expectations for subsequent budgets, so the publisher may wish to make additional capital expenditures in a particularly profitable year to manage those future expectations.

As the review of budgets is important to the ongoing health of a title, it is usual that such meetings will take place on a monthly basis and be attended by the publisher, sales director and editor at least, along with any other managers on the magazine such as circulation directors and marketing managers where appropriate. The function of such a meeting, as well as reviewing what has happened previously, should be to remind those managers of the importance of remaining in control of their expenses but also seek to provide useful ideas for future developments.

## Financing a new title or acquisition

For publishers seeking to start up a new title, whether as a first step into publishing or as part of business expansion that may also include acquisition of a competitor's magazines, the question of finding enough capital to finance the operation is the most important one.

The first step is to prepare a business plan, typically consisting of the following sections:

- Executive summary: this states what you want from the business – who your audience will be, how you hope to establish a profitable title in the marketplace and what you are looking for in terms of investment.
- A description of the industry you will be working for – for example, a particular professional sector if you are launching a B2B title, as

well as the operations for producing and distributing a magazine, how it will be sold and also any legal forms, whether this is sole proprietorship, a partnership or part of a corporation.

- A market analysis, indicating why there might be an audience for this type of magazine and, ideally, the results of research carried out to discover what type of magazine proposed readers would be looking for.

- A competitive analysis that outlines other players in this particular field and provides an account of how this new title will be different and why it is needed.

- An account of how the business will be run – for example, the structure of editorial, sales and circulation departments outlined in this and the next chapter – and how it will develop. For example, if the market for one type of magazine typically sustains sales of 50,000 to 100,000 copies sold on the newsstand and/or by subscription per year, you would need to indicate how you would achieve similar distributions. In addition, potential investors would want to know what plans there are to develop the business for future growth. As such, a design and development plan would need to deal with product, market and organisation development.

- Financial data, outlining the expenses and capital requirements. The elements outlined in the preceding section on magazine budgets would need to be analysed here, to demonstrate how much you think it would cost to run a magazine and what projections for income would be.

At all stages, independent legal and financial advice is always recommended, providing a perspective on what is feasible for a new launch or acquisition. The options then open to many publishers include:

- Senior debt finance: traditional secured bank loans, typically short term and paid back from a company's cash flow over three to five years.

- Venture capital or private equity: the investor takes a stake in the equity of the firm in return for the initial cash investment. Future earnings rather than current cash flow will repay the debt, and the investor will usually seek to recoup costs through selling the business or a stock market flotation.

- Internal investment: for large publishers, part of the profits from other operations are used to launch new titles, and in some cases a title may change owners due to such things as a senior management buyout.

- Government-backed finance: this can consist of grants or small firms loans that are often extremely useful for very small operations, and banks are able to advise on the various grants and loans available throughout the EU.

When approaching potential investors, a major concern will not just be the product itself and the possibilities of growth, but also the strength of a management team. If at some stage a publisher wishes to sell or buy a title, then they should also employ a broker who is knowledgeable about the magazine market (details for which can be found via the PPA) to evaluate properly the value of a title and negotiate any deals, a tax accountant to ensure that they can take full advantage of tax breaks, and a commercial lawyer with media experience.

# 3
# Attracting interest and circulation

Before a national commercial magazine can be published, the parent company must find a distributor willing to take on board the expensive prospect of shipping large quantities of bulky magazines to a huge number of retail outlets around the country. A publisher will have to demonstrate to the wholesaler that its title has a respectable chance of generating sufficient sales to make the venture worthwhile before work begins on editorial production: without a distribution deal, it makes little sense to invest in other areas such as editorial.

Two ways in which magazines attract interest to their title is by the creation of a 'dummy', a mock-up of the magazine that can give a distributor a feel for the title, and a media pack, a promotional document that provides potential advertisers with information about the publication and its readers.

Students creating a magazine with a limited circulation will not require a magazine dummy, and it is unlikely that they will require a media pack. And yet the process of creating the latter, in particular, is an immensely rewarding task and one that can demonstrate the relevant steps of researching a particular market. As such this chapter, after outlining the typical elements required in a media pack and their significance, will conclude with a project to produce such a pack that will offer a step-by-step guide to researching a particular market.

## Market research and registering a title

Until the arrival of the Internet and digital television, magazines comprised the pre-eminent medium for reaching niche audiences. In the UK, for example, and chosen entirely at random, there is a weekly magazine for fleet vehicle managers (*Fleet News*), a craft title for those interested in creating objects from card or paper (*PaperCraft Inspirations*), and a monthly that advises the pet industry (*Pet Product Marketing*). It is easy to find obscure titles that could be mocked as unbelievably arcane, but the fact is that once you move beyond the 100 top-selling WH Smith titles, the chances are that there is a magazine that is aimed at your very specific profession or interest.

The trend in the past couple of decades, particularly with the rise of the B2B sector, has been to target ever more clearly defined target markets. Obviously, there is the occasional launch that goes for a mass market, such as the men's weeklies *Nuts* and *Zoo*, but more generally new titles are aimed at a niche market based on what competing companies are producing or current trends.

The starting point for researching magazine markets is BRAD (British Rates and Data), a media directory published by Emap that also includes a range of online services (www.brad.co.uk/intelligence). In appearance, BRAD looks like a telephone directory that lists the vast majority of newspapers and magazines printed in the UK, organising them into sections such as aeronautics and music. It is primarily aimed at advertisers, in that it includes information on rates for all titles carrying advertising in the UK, but is also incredibly useful for anyone looking to set up a new title or wishing to know more about British media.

## Distribution and circulation

Getting a national magazine into a substantial proportion of the estimated 53,000 retail outlets that sell newspapers and magazines in the UK is no small task (and even more complex in the US, where there are more than 125,000 outlets), yet it is only one part of the job of a circulation director.

In addition to dealing with distributors who arrange deals with wholesalers for storing copies and then ship these to newsagents, supermarkets and other stores, he or she will have to ensure that subscriptions are managed efficiently and look for new potential readers, as well as determine how many copies of a magazine need to be printed. As such, this is one of the most important roles in magazine production and one that works in close association with the publisher.

In particular, the circulation director must combine a knowledge of finance with direct marketing and database management. Should circulation fall below the rate base over a period of time, advertisers are likely to want a discount – and should the circulation continue to fall over time it will be seen that the magazine is losing its appeal and is in trouble.

While there were more than 40,000 independent news outlets in 2006, the huge change in retail sales in recent years has been the rise of the supermarkets such as Tesco and Sainsbury's: complementing the 500 or so WH Smith retail branches in the UK, the 6,000 chain-owned stores now account for approximately 50 per cent of sales according to the PPA.

It is not realistic that every store carries every title in substantial numbers (which would be extremely wasteful), and so the task of distributors is to manage the number of copies throughout the sale period to ensure optimum sales. In general, for a magazine to be considered a success, launch issues will be expected to sell half of the supply, with a pattern being established within the first six months and 60 per cent performance considered a decent rate.

As new titles are only launched on a sale or return (SoR) basis, unsold copies are returned to the wholesaler with some being stored to provide back issues and the rest being pulped. This is in contrast to firm sales where the buyer pays for an issue whether it is sold or not.

The cover price tends to be split 50 per cent to the publisher, and 25 per cent going to the retailer, with the remainder divided between the wholesaler and distributor. Factors such as carriage costs and cover price will affect this division, and in some cases to ensure that a new title is carried by major high street retailers a publisher/distributor will negotiate a higher revenue return for the company selling the title.

In addition, for efficient sales (as well as monitoring), magazines need to be issued with a bar code: to do this, each title needs a unique ISSN (International Standard Serial Number) code, which can be obtained free of charge from the British Library, and then a bar code sourced through suppliers who maintain a list with the PPA.

## The distribution process

There are five layers in the distribution of a magazine: publisher, distributor, wholesaler, retailer, reader. After a magazine has been printed it is taken by the distributor to a depot (occasionally more than one) and from there sent out to the wholesaler network. While it is possible for a publisher to undertake their own distribution, this is incredibly difficult at a national level in a highly competitive market. Alternatively, specialist titles may engage in 'affinity sales', whereby the magazine is sold in a sympathetic outlet, for example, music magazines in music shops.

Publishers will usually work through a wholesale distributor, of which the market leaders are WH Smith (with 39 per cent market share in 2006), Menzies Distribution (27 per cent, but with a monopoly in Scotland) and Dawson News (19 per cent). Wholesalers, of which there are about 185 in the UK, most of them owned by these three companies, generally operate within a defined area in the country and typically distribute magazines to between 400 and 500 retail outlets.

As magazines can go on sale on any date chosen by the publisher, the distributor liaises with the publisher and printer in advance to determine a date when copies can be shipped across the wholesale network – which means that publication schedules have to be adhered to. The printer will prepare a pre-determined number of bundles of magazines that are then taken by the publisher: carriage costs from warehouse to wholesaler typically account for between one and three per cent of the cover price: from the wholesaler, copies can then be sent out to individual retail outlets.

Sometimes the same distributor will also be responsible for sending out subscription copies to readers. Alternatively, publishers can use what is known as a 'fulfilment bureau' to handle subscriptions or deal with these in-house. One service available to distributors and publishers is Presstream, a Royal Mail service that offers discounts for publications that exceed volumes of 1,000 per mailing and contain a minimum of one-sixth editorial content. More information on Presstream can be found at royalmail.com.

## Paid and controlled circulation and subscription

The main ways in which magazines reach their customers are via paid copies, controlled circulation and subscription. The most common way for consumer titles is to be sold via newstrade, whether in a retail outlet such as a newsagent or supermarket or a more unusual venue such as a festival or trade show. These are single-copy sales, and while they are responsible for the vast majority of consumer title sales this is not the case for many B2B magazines – nor, indeed, for the highest circulating magazines not aimed at those working in a specific profession or trade.

The difference can be seen by comparing figures for the top circulating versus top paid for consumer titles according to ABC for the six months to July 2007.

**Table 3.1** UK top ten circulating titles, July 2007

| Title | Average circulation per issue |
| --- | --- |
| Sky the Magazine | 7,002,232 |
| Asda Magazine | 2,743,005 |
| Tesco Magazine | 2,419,083 |
| The National Trust Magazine | 1,709,112 |
| Sainsbury's Fresh Ideas | 1,473,800 |
| What's On TV | 1,437,650 |
| TV Choice | 1,353,436 |
| Northern and Shell Women's Weeklies | 1,350,801 |
| The Somerfield Magazine | 1,244,715 |
| Radio Times | 1,082,338 |

**Table 3.2** UK top ten paid titles, July 2007

| Title | Average circulation per issue |
| --- | --- |
| What's On TV | 1,437,650 |
| TV Choice | 1,353,436 |
| Northern and Shell Women's Weeklies | 1,350,801 |
| Radio Times | 1,082,338 |
| Take a Break | 1,027,013 |
| Reader's Digest | 717,285 |
| BBC pre-school magazines | 654,880 |
| Closer | 614,141 |
| Heat | 598,623 |
| Saga Magazine | 610,771 |

As has been discussed in a previous chapter, these figures demonstrate the importance of TV titles and the women's market for consumer magazines, but what is significant here is the fact that five of the top ten circulating titles in the UK are not single-copy sales, but distributed freely in retail outlets (the supermarket titles) or are sent to subscribers as part of a more general package (as in the case of *Sky the Magazine* and *The National Trust Magazine*).

Subscriptions themselves divide into two categories: there are paid for subscriptions where any subscriber can purchase multiple issues of a magazine for a set period, and controlled subscriptions, where the magazine is sent out to a pre-selected audience, usually for free. This is the case with the Sky and National Trust titles, but is actually much more common in the B2B sector where readers will be sent a magazine because of their profession.

Controlled circulation, then, is really a feature that affects business titles – and it is not hard to see why. The potential readership for a consumer title is huge, but simply listing everyone who has visited their GP in the past 12 months is unlikely to generate much interest from advertisers, whereas the 35,000 plus readers of *Doctor*, distributed to those GPs for free by Reed Business Information Limited, will be seen as an extremely valuable market.

Unlike the newspaper industry, where there remains a fairly healthy appetite for free trade sheets such as *The Metro*, giving away consumer magazines for free is uneconomic: it is paid readership that counts. There are some exceptions, for example, bulk sales where discounted copies are sold to a business such as a hotel or airline that gives away copies to its customers, but this affects newspapers more than magazines.

By contrast, while the potential audience for B2B titles is much smaller (usually measured in the tens rather than hundreds of thousands), it is much more lucrative because of the specialist nature of a particular group. *Contract Journal*, another Reed title, may only have a circulation of 30,000 in the audit period up to June 2006, but the fact that well over a third of that readership could be identified as building and civil engineering contractors, with the remainder divided between other types of engineer and subcontractor, means that potential advertisers will be very sure of the type of person interested in reading that magazine – and in their products.

Paid circulation will, of course, make a valuable contribution to the revenues of a magazine, and paid subscription indicates an intention on the part of a subscriber to read the magazine regularly. This is important to advertisers who are more likely to consider that readership as loyal and attentive, but in specialist markets with much smaller audiences (typically measured in the tens of thousands in the UK and below 200,000 in the US), it is often more cost-effective to send out a controlled circulation title for free.

## The subscription base

When creating a subscription base, there are several possibilities open to a circulation director: the two most common ones come from offers within the magazine, or a direct mail promotion. Both will typically offer a reduced price to subscribers, as well as some other sort of promotional offer (such as a free gift), and direct mail shots will cost even more: it is usually assumed that only one to two per cent of those contacted in this way will respond, so it can cost a significant amount to attract each subscriber who will receive the magazine at a reduced rate.

Why, then, do publishers persist with subscription? Partly this is because some of those costs will be recouped on savings made by not making payments to the retailer, but, more importantly, subscription guarantees readership for a period of time. Single-sales, particularly of consumer magazines, can be greatly affected by seasonal variables such as the weather and holidays, whereas subscriptions tend to be constant. Indeed, with the move towards extra discounts for direct debit customers, the chances are that it takes more effort for a reader to cancel their subscription than let it continue and so this provides a more solid base for publishers.

Direct mailing – and indeed subscription lists more generally – bring with them particular legal requirements and obligations. The 1998 Data Protection Act means that individuals have to give their express permission for sensitive information (such as race or politics) to be stored, and transferring information abroad, particularly outside the EU, is particularly difficult.

The Direct Marketing Association (www.dma.org.uk) also produces a code of best practice, covering email and SMS as well as postal marketing:

this outlines legal requirements, such as the ability of members of the public to remove their names from direct marketing mailings, as well as complaints procedures and best practice for collecting and keeping data. These legal considerations will be considered more fully in Chapter 7.

In addition to direct mailing and magazine promotions, Internet and email mailings are of course much more common (but also tend to be less useful because of the general bane of spam), as well as inserts or advertisements in other titles.

## Successful subscription marketing

In addition to providing a steady revenue stream for publishers, subscribers are often important in terms of offering potentially detailed profiles about readers. In addition to the relatively straightforward but valuable data about where readers live, their occupations and other demographic information, subscribers are often asked by publishers to participate in reader feedback surveys, offering insights into what is popular within a particular issue of a magazine and what does not work. As subscribers will have already staked an interest in that title, they are also seen as being more responsive to further promotions and ancillary sales.

Yet for the circulation director and publisher, pursuing successful sub-scription marketing is not automatically straightforward. As has already been pointed out, gaining subscribers often costs money, and the need to raise circulation will not always be consistent with the demand to increase subscription revenues (something which is very similar with regard to cover price promotions: it is often very easy to sell more copies by dropping the cover price, but doing this too much simply becomes unprofitable).

As such, when working on a strategy to promote subscriptions, a publishing company must first take into account the basics of how the promotion will take place (inside the magazine, email, direct mailing and so on), but also other factors that may encourage a reader to take up the offer – for example, a price discount or free gift. With regard to payment, a so-called 'hard offer' requires payment with the subscription, while a 'soft offer' allows for later payment, and the publisher will need to consider options such as direct debit and credit/debit cards as well as cheques. Other promotional offers can include developing a special relationship with subscribers – a feature common in the B2B sector is to allow these readers access to restricted information on a web site, for example.

One technique to attract new readers is to offer a risk-free trial period where, if they are not happy, they can receive their money back without a quibble. This refund is unlikely to be taken up by most potential subscribers, but offers a sense of security. In addition to attracting new customers, the circulation director will wish to consider how best to continue those subscriptions. Conversion refers to those customers who repeat business after the initial offer, while renewal is used to describe those who continue to maintain their subscription. As attracting new readers costs money, conversion and renewal rates are extremely important to a publisher, so the timing of reminder letters as well as offers for 'early-bird' renewals are also important.

## Newsstand sales

While subscriptions are important for a wide range of magazines – essential for controlled circulation titles – there are many, particularly consumer magazines, that rely on single-copy sales at the newsstand. These range from small, independent newsagents to sections of large supermarkets, although sometimes titles will be sold in other retail outlets that do not treat such sales as their primary concern, for example, music stores which tend to stock a number of music magazines.

When a distributor determines how many copies to deliver to each part of the country, which are then shipped to the wholesaler network, the number of copies delivered is sometimes referred to as the 'draw', while the number of copies sold is the 'sell-through'. As previously noted, the publisher can expect 50 per cent of the cover price, but retailers may also charge extra for special promotions – for example, ensuring the full cover of the magazine will be on display.

In recent years, the sale of magazines (as with other consumer commodities) has been revolutionised by Electronic Point of Sale (EPoS). Work begun by Coopers and Lybrand in 1997 in association with the PPA and Association of Newspaper and Magazine Wholesalers (ANMW) set out to investigate how waste could be reduced where typically magazine sell-through is only half the potential draw. However, while the benefits of EPoS have been very clear in the supermarket sector and major high street retailers such as WH Smith, it has not extended by any means to all independent newsagents and, in any case, there is a danger that wholesalers and distributors can over-react to a very volatile market where sales of magazines vary greatly from issue to issue.

This leads on to what Daly, Henry and Ryder call the 'cover as newsstand variable': perhaps the single biggest factor affecting single-copy sales is the way an individual cover is perceived.

> The variables that can affect the sale of a copy of a magazine are many and include the draw, the cover lines for articles within that issue, cover price, competition from similar maga- zines on the same display rack, seasonality, issue promotion and the number of days the publication remains on sale. But no variable is as important as the cover. Unfortunately, designing and creating an attention-getting cover is an inexact science. A cover must be viewed as it might appear on a newsstand, amidst a mass of other magazines of every imaginable design and color.
>
> (Daley et al. 1997: 102)

Thus, as they point out, the current appetite for celebrity means that famous figures are more likely to appear than ever before – but this is itself no assurance that a magazine will achieve an improved sell-through. In addition, the economics of the draw means that at a certain point limitations start to kick in: just because a magazine with a draw of 200,000 sells half of the copies in circulation, increasing the number to 400,000 will not guarantee sales of 200,000. Overestimating the sell-through on a print run is costly.

Similarly, cover price is a significant factor, and this is largely determined by the competition. While the recently burgeoning chat magazine market (including titles such as *Now!* and *Pick Me Up*) has titles that all sell around the £1 range, IT and gaming magazines will typically sell for anywhere between £4 and £6 for monthlies – but only if they are perceived to offer added value in the form of free software, and this sector has shrunk considerably over the past five years.

Seasonality affects some publications considerably, with travel titles picking up before holiday seasons, while more business-oriented maga- zines tend to suffer during the summer. Finally, days on sale can have an impact: ideally, publishers would like their title to remain on sale for

30 or 31 days during the month, but retailers may pull a magazine from the newsstand to make way for a faster selling title if it is not selling enough.

## Auditing and sales verification

Until advertising became important for generating revenue, there was no attempt to verify how many copies of a particular magazine were sold. The Audit Bureau of Circulations (ABC, www.abc.org.uk) was founded in 1914 and the Business Publications Audit, Inc. (BPA, www.bpaww.com) in 1931; each was set up by groups of advertisers and publishers to provide an impartial and external mechanism that would audit magazine sales and standardise how information was presented.

Both of these companies perform a similar function, the main difference being that while ABC has a much larger membership overall, BPA has traditionally performed more strongly in the business sector. The classification systems used by each company were merged in the mid-1980s, making it easier to compare results across both.

Circulation is initially reported in a publisher's statement (in the US referred to as a 'pink sheet'), the best estimate of sales in a six-month period from January through June, or July through December. Auditors then analyse that statement for accuracy and issue their own report. The importance of this process is that it helps advertisers determine not only the number of copies sold, but also if the manner in which they are sold meets their expectations. For example, if an advertiser deals only in the UK, then if large numbers of a title are sold abroad this may affect how they deal with a magazine. It is also worth noting that magazine circulation is very different to a magazine's audience which will usually be much larger, the assumption being that more than one person reads each copy.

A circulation statement contains information on average paid circulation, both from the newsstand for single-sale copies and subscriptions (including sponsored subscriptions, that is quantities of 11 or more), and non-paid circulation. In addition to the controlled circulation discussed previously, this can include consumer titles that send out copies of a magazine at no charge to public places or individuals with an affiliated interest.

Over a six-month period, this then produces the total average circulation, the number of copies sold in total divided by the number of issues over that period. ABC has particular rules about which copies can be included: for example, a publisher must provide information about where the magazine will be sold, as well as analysis of individual subscriptions. In addition, the publisher must provide a reader with the opportunity to opt-out of a subscription – a reflection of the fact that unscrupulous publishers can inflate their circulation figures by sending out free copies that a reader no longer requires.

## Additional factors

Certain other factors are taken into account when auditing how many copies of a magazine are sold. When a subscription runs out, it is not uncommon for a publisher to continue to send out copies: how many of these arrears, or post-expiration copies, can be sent is limited depending on the length of subscription, yet it is often a useful tactic not simply to inflate figures but also as part of a renewal strategy to tempt back readers. Auditors also take into account 'premium incentives' – add-ons that can be sent out to attract readers: these may be editorial (such as reprints of past content from a magazine in a booklet form) or non-editorial (free gifts).

Publishers that wish to verify their circulation become members of the ABC or BPA and then submit new titles for registration. After downloading forms to enter relevant information and paying fees (for example, £929 to audit a consumer title, plus other fees for inspection and annual membership), a certificate is issued after six months or one year.

During this period sales can fluctuate considerably: some of this may be due to decisions made by the publisher, for example, to target a particular group of people to change the composition of an audience, as a response to changing fashions and fads, or due to material costs such as paper. More often, issue-by-issue circulation is affected by other factors, including seasonality (holiday periods may be particularly good for one type of publication, but less so for others), popularity of certain covers, harsh weather and changes in the economy which influence overall spending.

## ABCE

One of the biggest changes in recent years is the importance of the Internet to magazine publishers. While the importance of this can be exaggerated for certain sectors (such as consumer magazines), for newspapers and the B2B industry, web sites and other electronic distribution systems such as email newsletters have developed into an important part of reaching their audience.

ABC Electronic (ABCE, www.abce.org.uk) was established in 1996 to provide a similar service for web sites that could verify audiences to potential advertisers, and BPA followed suit with BPA Interactive Accreditation in 2007. While these sites had long claimed that it was much easier to measure such things as hits and unique visits to their sites, a lack of standards meant it was difficult to measure performance.

In addition, because of the activities of search engine bots or crawlers, software that trawls the web looking for pages to add to databases, a considerable amount of online activity is not generated by people. ABCE set up an agreed way of identifying visits, what it calls the Industry Agreed Metrics, that measures the following areas:

- **Page impressions or volume:** how many hits or times a page is loaded in a browser.
- **Unique users or 'audience reach':** individuals accessing a site measured through such things as unique IP addresses or registered user names.
- **Frequency:** how long visitors spend on each page.
- **Ad impressions:** similar to page impressions, how many banner or text ads are viewed on a page.
- **Ad clicks:** the response to advertising measured by users clicking through on an advert rather than simply viewing it.

As well as web sites, ABCE can audit email and SMS distribution, and even chat sites and video or audio streams. By subscribing to the service, publishers can offer an industry-agreed standard of verification of circulation to advertisers comparable to their print services.

## Creating a media pack

A media pack is aimed principally at advertisers and potential investors in a title and, typically, provides the following information:

**Editorial statement:** This will also often be referred to as a brand statement, and is intended to provide a concise view of the magazine's status, ambitions and purpose. Sometimes this will include a brief outline of the typical content of an issue or recent features, as well as seeking to position the title in terms of an editorial stance (for example, whether it is combative, investigative, informative, the reader's friend and so on). In attempting to outline the aims and ambitions that establish the core brand, this is the opportunity to establish what may be distinctive about a particular title.

**Market and readership:** In seeking to attract potential advertisers, a media pack often includes demographic information (age, gender, socio-economic status) and details specific to a particular group (for example, if they share an interest in urban music, are women in their twenties, or are an audience largely comprised of flight professionals. In some cases, a media pack may refer to competitors in the field (although usually only in the vaguest terms) to indicate what is different about this particular title.

**Figure 3.1** *Financial World* media pack

**Verified/estimated circulation:** As has already been established, the significance of auditing is that it verifies circulation, but some smaller titles that cannot afford or choose not to go down the auditing route may offer estimated circulation figures. Media packs will also often distinguish between paid circulation and readership, the latter usually being between two to four times the size of the former (the assumption being that a magazine will be passed around after it is bought).

**Advertising rates:** One of the principal functions of a media pack is to provide information on advertising costs, which will normally be provided in the form of a rate card. At its simplest, this will break down ad rates based on size (so that a double-page spread is more expensive than a single page of display advertising which, in turn, costs more than a half page and so on), but larger titles will also typically have a more complex set of prices. Position is important, so that adverts near the front of a magazine, or those facing suitable editorial content (facing matter), cost more than those towards the end, with the most expensive rates reserved for inside or back covers. In addition, some titles will offer discounts on advertising that is bought over a longer period.

**Additional information:** While editorial and advertising material tends to be common to all media packs, sometimes they may include additional information on such things as distribution (if a title is distributed via special arrangements, such as through particular shops or trade shows, or subscriptions), online versions which are becoming particularly important to magazine publishers, research or other business services which are especially significant to the B2B sector, as well as links to trade shows, conferences or syndication rights.

# 4
# Copy and editorial

So far we have looked at the business and context of magazines. Now it is time to turn to the actual production of a magazine, beginning with its written content. Subsequent chapters will consider the role of art and design in the production process. Here we shall focus on the typical structure of an editorial department, as well as some of the essential elements for creating good content based around preparation, commissioning and checking/subbing material. Some other features, particularly with regard to ethical and legal factors that have to be considered by editors, are considered in Chapter 7.

## The role of the editor

Journalistic skills and management are key to the role of the editor. While he or she has to engage with every level of production throughout the magazine, it is also important that the editor has the maturity to take legal and moral responsibility for everything that appears in the title and can delegate the necessary tasks to ensure that it is published on deadline. In addition to working within the title, the editor is also the main representative, alongside the publisher, of the magazine to the outside world: for readers in particular, he or she will often be the person most associated with the brand, and so will have to provide leadership to his or her team to shape its purpose and mission.

Ideally, the editor will have worked in just about every aspect of journalism, whether editorial work for news, features and reviews or as a sub-editor. In practice, he or she will only have fulfilled a few of these aspects, but still the editor needs to understand how each area of their title functions and how to bring them together into a complete package.

On smaller titles, with very small editorial teams, the editor may also be a de facto contributor to each and every section, while on larger publications he or she may delegate responsibilities to section editors. Nonetheless, it is still important for the editor to be able to write copy, sub-edit and draft headlines or captions: with this comes confidence but also an understanding of how these different elements work.

## Routes into editing

The two routes into editing tend to involve those who come from a writing background and those who come from production. The journalistic requirements for a reporter or feature writer can be very different to those of a sub-editor: a writer will need to substantiate the facts of their story and collate together all their sources, engaging in research to produce the best copy that they can write.

A sub, on the other hand, is more concerned with clarity and consistency, and very often that content 'fits' with other parts of the magazine and deadlines. In addition, subs, working closely with a design department, have to pay attention to those elements that make a title or article stand out – the eye-grabbing headline or well-placed picture, cover lines and standfirsts that will make a reader on the newsstand pick up the magazine in the first place.

The skills that come from production are immensely useful to an editor in that they enable him or her to see the shape of the magazine, how word counts are transformed into columns and pages that, in turn, become sections and finally the whole product combining editorial and advertising in a format that is most appealing to an audience. In addition, working closely with a production department will provide an editor with a clearer understanding of the technicalities of design, printing and distribution. He or she will know what can or cannot work – the nuts and bolts of which will be left to the subs and production editors.

Those editors who come from a writing background, however, will also have other, extremely important abilities. Being an editor means that you are not – should not – be bound to the desk: success in this area comes from speaking to people, and reporters and writers will have to interview subjects on a daily basis, building up contacts, working with PR agencies, dealing with clients and strangers. The editor has to be willing to speak to anyone (or have very good reasons not to), as he or she is the public face of the story.

Likewise, while a good sub will recognise those visual and verbal clues that appeal to readers, a reporter has the nose for a good story and needs constantly to come up with new ideas. When he or she has the skill to turn this into a compelling narrative, this is something that can be taken to another level by the editor who needs to craft a similar narrative for each issue of the magazine, or even the brand itself.

The best editors will combine elements of both writing and production: the demands of a deadline or a particular layout should not be allowed to dilute or distort the impact of a good writer's work – in the worst of cases the need to make a story fit a column could end up with erroneous statements that are potentially libellous. At the same time, a talented freelance may not have the reader fully in mind.

## Editing and management

Beyond these writing and technical skills, it should never be forgotten that editing is also a managerial role – something that can often hinder those who have worked their way up the ranks and developed an 'us and them' mentality with regard to the management. The level of management given to an editor will vary from title to title, but it will nearly always involve some level of budget control, such as freelance payments and expenses, legal decisions with regard to what will appear in the magazine, people skills to ensure that a team pulls together to produce the magazine, and usually responsibility for hiring and firing staff.

As well as being the main figurehead who bridges magazine staff and readers, an editor has an important part to play within a magazine as the bridge between editorial and other departments. While magazine editors often wish to stand apart from the business of publishing, this is unlikely to be a successful strategy in today's commercial market.

## Editors and publishers

The editor must be willing to engage with the publisher, marketing departments and (often the most tricky) the media sales team. While a good editor will have a vision of where the magazine is going – and must be willing to stand up for it against the demands of a publisher and advertisers if he or she sees that they will affect readers of the magazine adversely – ultimately the best brands are those in which all aspects of magazine publishing and production work in some sort of harmony.

As publishers often come from a sales background, there can be a sense of disdain towards editorial staff who are seen as somehow 'protected' from the harsh economic realities of magazine sales. (In practice, editors may also prefer a degree of this disdain – publishers who come from editorial may be a much worse burden in terms of their levels of interference.)

Editors who neglect commercial concerns are liable to drag their title into financial difficulties – for example, by alienating too many advertisers or readers; at the same time, an editor who is concerned only with profit above all things is unlikely to produce a magazine that can be trusted by the general public. The editor must always be willing to stand up for the interests of his or her staff, to ensure that the pages they create and which, ultimately, sell the magazine, can follow the route that will always take into account what attracts readers to the title in the first place.

This brings us to the final role of the editor, as an advocate for the reader. He or she should provide leadership, both internally to members of an editorial team, and also externally in terms of having something to say rather than simply following fashions. At the same time, an editor who neglects his or her readership to follow personal hobby horses could soon be presiding over a rapidly declining circulation.

There is a danger in all this of becoming too oriented towards a 'focus-group' mentality, in which no editorial decision is made without consulting readers in some way: an experienced editor will often have good hunches about what the public wants, rather than what it thinks it wants. Nonetheless, the writer (and it is usually editors coming from a writing background who display this tendency) who thinks only of what he or she wants to say without regard for the consequences is probably far too arrogant to lead a magazine.

## Editorial and production

The editor, as outlined above, will have responsibility for two main areas of the magazine, namely, editorial (writing) and production, incorporating subbing and design. If there is no substantial design work to be done, and a title does not appear too frequently, it is not uncommon for an editor to commission a layout artist to produce a template for a magazine which he or she can complete for each issue.

It is much more common, however, for magazines to work with an in-house team comprising several members of staff. At the smallest, these may be specialist newsletters comprising one or two writers with design being handled by a centralised production department, with slightly larger titles consisting of an editor and editorial assistant, plus an art-editor and sub-editor (both of whom may be full- or part-time). For such publications, commissioning is handled by the editor and most of the actual content is likely to be produced by freelances, with the assistant ensuring that administrative tasks such as dealing with invoices and taking calls are dealt with.

## Section editors

For regular monthly magazines with substantial pagination, a dedicated, larger editorial team becomes a necessity – not least because there must be sufficient staff to cover holidays. While the editor provides overall leadership and is responsible for planning the flow of copy, much of the day-to-day administration will be delegated to a deputy editor and/or section editors.

Who these editors are will vary according to the makeup of the magazine, for example, a news editor if news stories are important, a features editor or number of features editors covering different aspects of a magazine's makeup. Such staff will be responsible for commissioning content for each issue and will generally be in more constant contact with freelances. In addition, they will be delegated work from the editor that involves going out and speaking to people about the magazine: a music reviews editor, for example, will need to attend events that involve the music industry.

Working under these editors will be reporters and staff writers whose responsibilities are more generally limited to producing copy, although as they tend to be assigned a 'beat' – a topic to keep abreast of – such writers will be expected to maintain a list of contacts, attend press conferences where necessary, and interview subjects for their articles.

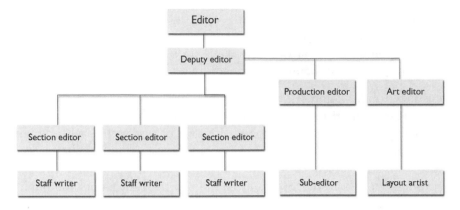

**Figure 4.1** Typical editorial structure of a large magazine

For a medium- to large-sized magazine, the production department will usually consist of some form of managing or production editor alongside an art department. The production editor (considered in more detail in Chapter 6) has the important job of ensuring that the trains run on time: once a schedule is agreed for production, he or she will need to liaise with departments to make sure that, for example, copy comes in when required and that it is subbed and returned to editors for a final check. As he or she often has control of the flat-plan, another important task will be liaising with the advertising director: changes to the number of advertising pages coming in can have important consequences for how editorial is arranged.

While the production editor is usually in charge of sub-editors, alongside these there will often be an art department. The art editor has the main responsibility for the look and feel of a magazine, in conjunction with the editor, and will often be the manager of a team of graphic artists whose job it is to lay out pages and possibly produce graphics. In addition, he or she will commission illustrations and photography. For multi-title companies, both elements of production (subbing and design) are often centralised, with teams working across several magazines.

Although not part of the in-house team, a final important constituent for most titles is its stable of freelances. Any editor will seek to build up a collection of reliable writers, designers and photographers that he or she can call on to provide content for different issues. The virtue of using freelances is flexibility: if budgets are tight, content can be cut back and then increased if the demand grows. The disadvantages can include less control over work (which is why the issue of reliability becomes so important), and potential difficulties regarding rights over content.

## Editorial planning

The editorial process can be incredibly complex for magazines with large teams and substantial numbers of contributors, and it is the task of the production editor and editor to work out a schedule that can bring together all elements of a title into a finished product. Copy and graphics must be sourced, content checked for quality and accuracy, laid out and subbed in accordance with a house style, and the whole lot checked again before being despatched to a printer.

This is not a linear procedure, in that different people will be working on different parts of the magazine at the same time and passing content back and forth between them. Keeping track of this is much easier if there is a system in place to plan ahead.

The lead-in time for a monthly magazine, from the moment when articles are commissioned to when they appear in print, is typically around six weeks. The full process of creating a schedule will be discussed in Chapter 6 when dealing with the role of the production editor: here we will concentrate on the task of planning for editorial.

## The editorial calendar

Before commissioning can take place, the editor and his or her team require a calendar, which will usually consist of several forms. Any title working in a particular market will have a set of annual events which are more or less fixed from year to year. For a fashion magazine, it will be the launch of new collections, for an automobile title there will be the big trade shows and registration changeovers. There are things throughout the year that readers will expect to be covered, and seasonal changes from summer to winter will affect what people are buying and looking for.

Onto these bare bones, an editor will then try to second-guess what will be significant in the market for the coming year. A 12-month calendar will only be sketchy, but when planning ahead for six months and three months, this will start to include more and more detail.

While long-term editorial planning is, to some degree, always a little futile in that fashions change, it is an attempt to make the unpredictable a little more routine and is also essential not merely for working out what contributions will be made by journalists and designers, but also for sales and marketing teams: if they have an idea of what will be appearing in the magazine three issues down the line, they can begin to contact potential advertisers and plan press releases.

By the time a three-month calendar is drawn up, planning for an issue will become much more serious. At the stage when one issue is being completed, commissioning editors will be thinking of who to approach not simply for the next magazine, but the one after that. The process of editorial planning will run more or less along the following lines.

- The first step will be a planning meeting of some sort with section editors, where ideas are discussed and names put forward. In addition, a tentative running order and estimate of pagination will be outlined.
- Commissioning editors locate suitable writers, photographers and so on and find out whether they will be willing to take on work. If so, a detailed brief is drawn up, alongside some form of letter of contract indicating terms and conditions (although, with regular contributors, this will probably be no more than an email indicating the price for the work). In-house writers will also be briefed on what they need to produce for the forthcoming issue.
- The production editor will draw up a flat-plan, a 'map' of the magazine that becomes extremely important for organising the workflow of the issue.
- When copy comes in, the copy-editing process begins: this used to involve filing away typescripts, but these days submissions will nearly always be in digital format – not simply for the convenience of delivery via email or on disk, but also because it is easier to strip out text from a word-processed document and lay it out in a DTP application such as QuarkXPress or Adobe InDesign.
- A commissioning editor will read through the article and ensure that it fulfils the brief: if not, it is sent back to the writer or passed along to someone in-house to rewrite. This is one reason why deadlines for submission must be early enough to allow time to adjust text – although if this is a common occurrence then the editor

must consider if he or she is clear enough when writing a brief, or whether it would be better to find new contributors. Sometimes, however, a rewrite is simply necessary: a freelance may follow a brief to the letter, but circumstances change and a story needs to be recast.

- When final copy is accepted, it is then passed to subs who read through looking for obvious errors and ensure that it is in accordance with the house style.
- The next stage is for copy to be laid out by designers, which will be covered in more detail in the next two chapters.
- After layout, copy is returned to subs for rechecking – an important part of the process: when a designer is working on a page, his or her main concern is to make it look as good as possible rather than read accurately. This is very often one of the stages where errors can creep in.

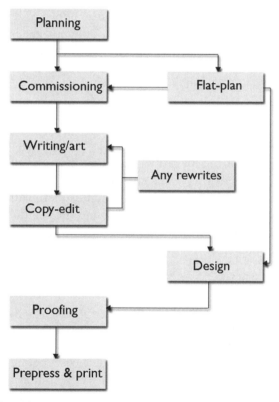

**Figure 4.2** The editorial workflow

- Once a feature has been subbed, it can be checked again by section editors and passed to the editor to be signed off. While some editors, particularly on large titles, may take a more hands-off approach to commissioning and large parts of the production process, it is important that they read through and sign off as much material as possible. Ultimately, if say an article is libellous, they will have responsibility for that material. The difficulty is that this can create a bottleneck in the process, with too much content waiting the final approval of a busy editor.

While this presents the editorial process in a fairly linear manner, it is important to reiterate that an ongoing title will stagger different parts of the flow of copy. For example, a features editor may start commissioning far in advance of the editor responsible for reviews, while the news editor will not find it to his or her advantage to start commissioning stories six weeks in advance of publication.

What this means is that the system outlined above will overlap with different sections of a magazine – and with different issues. At one part of the day, the production editor may be checking that copy is in for the feature section of the January issue and at another be finalising the subbing for news going into the December title.

## Flat-planning

A flat-plan is a map of the magazine, detailing where everything will go from the front cover to the back, and its preparation is an extremely important part of the editorial process. A flat-plan will show where editorial and advertising pages are allocated, and the pagination will often be worked out several months in advance as part of the budgeting process discussed in Chapter 2.

A flat-plan will be arranged into sections, with a minimum of four pages to each section (this being the number of pages that will be produced by one sheet of paper, depending on the printing process, with more common quantities being eight or sixteen). For the production editor, this is an important factor when planning magazine production: different sections can be sent off to start printing in some cases before the magazine is completed, so deadlines for such things as copy and layout have to be organised so that both editorial and advertising content comes in at the same time for each part of the magazine.

## Advertising and editorial

With regard to advertising, determining where ads appear within the title obviously has an impact on the amount of money paid. This can cause more than a little friction: advertisers generally want their display pages as near the front as possible (if the back and inside covers have already been sold), which is why so many magazines have pages of advertising before you hit any editorial. Unsurprisingly, they prefer their ads to face editorial rather than other advertisements, and will always wish to go on the right-hand page (the spot where the eye naturally falls on opening a magazine).

The temptation on the part of the publisher and sales department to push for as many right-hand pages as possible has to be resisted to some degree: too many ads on this side and readers may believe that the magazine has less editorial content than actually exists, making it bad value for money.

In addition, the presence of double-page editorial spreads allows art designers an opportunity to create something with a little more flair: when devising the flat-plan, the task for the editor, working in conjunction with the production editor and art editor, is to create some variety throughout the magazine, so that editorial does not always appear on single, left-hand pages and so looks very dull.

In American magazines, there is a tendency to put aside a portion in the centre of the magazine for editorial only, with no advertising, although this is less common in British titles. One effect of this is that a series of long features, which can be rather text heavy, is broken up so that the first few pages appear in the centre and the rest of the article is located at the end of the magazine.

In the UK, advertisements usually appear between articles and within them, sometimes creating a few problems as too many ads may disrupt a long feature; that said, too many one-page articles facing each other can be equally disconcerting, and so the placement of ads may be very useful from a design and editorial point of view in terms of helping to differentiate articles from each other.

While editorial pagination will be determined early on during the planning stage, advertising can be slightly more problematic: obviously, the publisher and advertising director will have a budget which determines the number of pages allocated to ads, but ads are usually sold in single

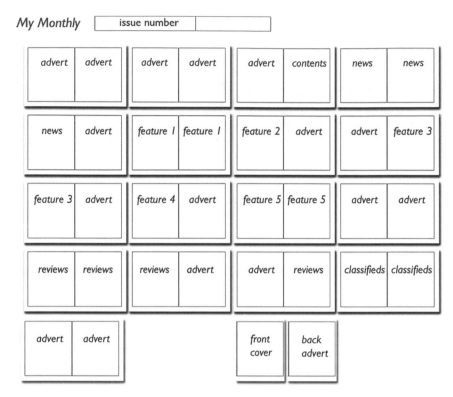

**Figure 4.3** A sample flat-plan

pages or double-page spreads. If the ratio of advertising to editorial is 40 : 60 (that is 40 pages of advertising against 60 pages of editorial), selling 42 pages means that there will be two pages less of editorial.

The amount of advertising sold tends to fluctuate throughout the year, and editors will need to establish reasonable limits against which the ratio of editorial pages can expand or decrease. If the allocation for advertising pages cannot be hit for some reason, this may leave an editor with the headache of a few extra pages to fill. When planning for this, editors may commission additional material that is not time-sensitive (and so can be carried across to the next issue), or have on hand 'house ads', advertisements for related magazines, that can be inserted into a blank space.

For this reason, a flat-plan is often an evolving rather than static map of the magazine – but to avoid a nervous breakdown the production editor will want it to remain as fixed as possible during the production cycle. Once it has been determined, copies of it will be distributed to the art department, section editors and advertising sales team.

## The post-mortem

While planning would seem logically to conclude with sending a magazine 'to bed', that is sending files or film to a printer, another important stage is the post-mortem. This is a meeting after the finished magazine has been received, where the editor and his or her team will consider the issue, discussing elements that worked or did not work so well. The aim of the post-mortem is to capitalise on successes and find out why particular failures may have happened and so prevent them occurring again.

## News

While news tends, unsurprisingly, to be associated with newspapers, it has an incredibly important role to play in a wide variety of magazines. While general men's and women's magazines probably do not really carry much news of importance – such things as celebrity events and gossip being dealt with on a more efficient basis by the tabloids, with their daily turnaround – other types of consumer magazines may inform their readers in a way that is not dealt with sufficiently by the daily press.

It is in B2B titles, however, that magazine news reporting probably really comes into its own: specialist titles for a particular industry or profession need to keep readers up to date with all that is happening, and this kind of expert information is seen as too rarefied to be dealt with in larger-circulation newspapers.

Hicks *et al.* (1999: 11) provide the most straightforward definition of news as that which is 'factual, new and interesting'. As such, it must provide information that, to readers at least, is unknown and which must also be of interest to them. A story on calls for an amnesty on financial clawback for missed targets for British dentists is unlikely to appeal to the nation as a whole, but is important enough to be a lead in *Dentistry Magazine* as it will affect a significant proportion of the audience.

This specificity is probably what distinguishes most magazine news journalism from newspaper news reporting. Obviously journalists on a daily will have a beat, specific areas that they need to report on such as crime or sport, but there is also the fact that readers browsing through different sections of a newspaper will have no, or very little, connection in terms of occupation, age, socio-economic status and interests.

## News for magazine audiences

By contrast, for all but the biggest-circulating consumer titles there will be something that ties a magazine to its audience very closely: for the readers of *Auto Express*, new car launches will be extremely important to just about everyone who opens its pages, while *The Lawyer Magazine* is very clearly aimed at a particular class of professionals. Indeed, for B2B titles it is often very sensible to make certain assumptions about the background of potential readers, for example, their level of education and expertise in a field, if the title does not wish to appear to talk down to them.

Magazines cannot expect to beat newspapers on topicality – even the schedule for weeklies means that they will not have the chance to get into print with regular scoops. However, what they often have is a level of expertise and knowledge about a particular field that is not matched by more generalist papers.

Scoops are not impossible: sometimes events of a much wider significance can be hidden away from the public gaze but are unearthed by a specialist journalist who has the contacts and knowledge to realise something important is going on. Of course, if a scoop does make it into a magazine before the papers and is relevant to a wider audience, editors of the dailies will soon take it up and start uncovering information that can be published more quickly.

The strength of magazines is that news can then lead into much longer features than are typically available for the newspaper format. As such, B2B titles especially can offer greater analysis and in-depth background to news events by drawing upon their links and sources within a particular industry.

## Writing magazine news

With the one (extremely important) proviso noted above about taking into account the particular nature of a magazine audience, many of the facets that go into writing news stories for magazines are very similar to those for other media such as newspapers. A news story should be well-crafted and also provide an angle, a point of view that establishes why a story makes sense.

This is not the same as propaganda: distorting facts so that they fit a particular purpose is, unfortunately, all too common in journalism and damages the profession. However, a good reporter always has a sense of why a particular story will be of interest to his readers, which in turn is linked to his or her news sense, the experience of knowing why some topics are appealing.

As mentioned previously, there are plenty of good books that will outline the qualities that comprise a good news story, so here we will concentrate simply on outlining the basics.

## The six questions and the news pyramid

If anyone knows anything about journalistic writing, it is probably the six questions that every opening paragraph should aspire to answer: who, what, why, where, how and when. Here is an example taken from the *UK Press Gazette*:

> Magazine publisher Hachette Filipacchi (UK) and chief executive Kevin Hand [WHO] are suing Haymarket Media for libel damages. [WHAT] The legal battle centres around a story in *Media Week* magazine [WHERE] in April, [WHEN] headed "Hachette faces an uncertain future". [WHY] And they are seeking an injunction banning repetition of the allegations made in the story. [HOW]

The six questions are a checklist, a means of providing relevant information as concisely as possible. The information they provide should appear throughout the story, although sometimes a particular element may not be as relevant: who and what are always essential, but the other questions may vary from piece to piece.

Another long-standing formula is the news pyramid, whereby points in a news story are made in descending order of importance. Thus essential details have to appear in the opening paragraph and additional information can then appear later in the story. The reason for this is twofold: sometimes sub-editors will need to cut a story and do not wish to worry about losing essential information; similarly, readers will often skim the beginnings of news stories to get up to speed, then finish reading once their curiosity is satisfied.

With these questions and the notion of the news pyramid in mind, the intro to a news story needs to grab a reader's attention and make sense to them instantly. It should convey the essential facts of a story and should be short – usual recommendations are between 20 and 30 words.

## Facts, claims and objectivity

Objectivity is often a touchstone of journalism, and one which raises considerable difficulties on a philosophical, practical and even political level. The question of whether a journalist can ever be truly objective is beyond the scope of this book, and merely selecting the facts as they appear important to the reporter, without any deliberate distortion of evidence, will often introduce an element of bias into a story.

However, on the practical level, the requirement to distinguish facts from claims is an essential journalistic skill. If reporting what purports to be a fact, this needs to be verified as much as humanly possible, as opposed to reporting what is said in speech or a written report. Thus, for example, the fact that a particular movie cost $200 million to make is relatively easy to check, but if someone interviewed for a story tells the reporter that it is the most expensive movie ever made, that is a claim that needs to be identified as such within the story.

When a claim is being presented, it should be clearly indicated: the source of the information should be given, although if this material comes from a press conference or routine interview those facts do not need to be pointed out. For written sources, however, some additional detail (the title of a report, for example) should be provided.

## Running stories, news style and structure

Running stories are extremely important in newspapers, where events in a significant case such as a murder inquiry may only unfold over a period of days or weeks. Repeating essential facts (such as the background of a key player) will become irritating very quickly. Periodicals which appear on a monthly or weekly basis may not suffer from this problem quite as much, but if a title is reporting regularly on a major issue that affects its target audience and which they are likely to remember, running or follow-up stories may omit background detail in subsequent issues.

When dealing with style, it is important to remember that news stories need to be as direct and vivid as possible. If the reader cannot determine the main points of a story in the opening paragraph, he or she is unlikely to read on. As news stories typically deal with events that have already happened, then it is normal for them to be told in the past tense. Occasionally, however, a news story will be told in the present tense to make it more vivid, moving to the past tense as the reporter provides factual details.

> Troopideas.com is not exactly 'MySpace for war fighters,' but it's a Web site that invites frontline troops to post their ideas for improving the combat experience. Engineers and developers then use Web 2.0 techniques such as mashups and wikis to turn those ideas into reality.
>
> (PC World)

Common styles to make a story more interesting include 'selling' the story – picking up a particular feature in the piece and telling readers why they need to know this fact – and a narrative style more usually found in fiction, establishing a colourful background to the bare facts of the story.

The virtues of both are that they can be more dramatic than the rather bald who, what, why, where, how and when formula, but the danger is that they can put off a reader, either by selling them a detail that does not interest them, or by failing to provide them with essential information that keeps them reading.

Another common technique is the 'delayed drop', usually indicated by the use of the word 'but', which indicates the tenor of the story is about to change in a vivid fashion. This, in turn, indicates the importance of building the structure of a news story. Where a delayed drop is not used, it is more usual to build the pyramid, retelling the short, punchy intro with more detail. Alternatively, the reporter may build up the story by providing the background events that led to the series of facts given in the first paragraph. As the story progresses, quotes and further supporting evidence can be introduced.

## The role of the news editor

While the business of spotting news is something that can be spread throughout an entire editorial team, in practice it is usual to have dedicated staff responsible for the news section of a magazine. For small titles, this may simply consist of a single reporter line-managed directly by the editor, but for magazines where news plays an important factor there may be a news editor running a small team.

The reason for separating news out from other sections is often due to the practicalities of magazine production as much as anything else. Features tend to be less time-specific than reviews which, in turn, go out of date less quickly than news. The production editor will probably be handling a series of deadlines for news stories that are much later in the cycle than those for features.

A good news editor does not merely wait for events to happen, but plans for them in advance. Certain events will affect readers, and while the outcome of these events cannot be known in advance, the fact that they will happen is clear. For example, large companies will make important announcements at major trade shows and may not release information in advance – but the editor knows that he or she needs a reporter there to feed back information.

In addition, writers need to contact industry figures to discover what is going on in the background, and very often PR departments will provide information under embargo, whereby a magazine has the essential facts but cannot report on them until a specified date. Background details to a news story can be written before the time-relevant material is made available.

One important task for the news editor is to encourage his or her staff to build up their contacts book. In addition, close attention should be paid to competitors – not to find out breaking stories (it is too late to do anything about them once they have been published) but to discover the sources that they use for information and to pursue them in future.

The starting point for a lot of stories is the press release, which typically is sent to the news editor. This type of material – increasingly in electronic form – can become overwhelming very easily (and the skill to writing a good press release very often matches that of writing a good news story in that you need to keep your reader engaged).

It is a depressing fact that staff cutbacks on a number of magazines often mean that such releases become the basis of a story – and, indeed, for a short caption story or minor column piece this is not in itself a problem: the magazine is passing on information, usually in a concentrated form, from companies and organisations. However, for bigger stories, such material should be used to provide contacts to follow up for the questions that a magazine's readers want answering – rather than as the opportunity simply for an organisation to tell only the answers that it wants to give.

## Features

In contrast to news, which tends to follow a number of fairly clearly defined formulas, magazine features are marked only by their variety. Features can range from short, photo-led articles with long captions (popular in celebrity magazines, for example), to detailed and densely researched articles that run for many pages throughout a title. The only constraint, as Sally Adams (Hicks *et al.* 1999) points out, is to write for the publication and its readers.

Bearing in mind this variety, the main types of features tend to consist of: profiles (of an individual or group/organisation); product round-ups (of the type commonly found in *Which?* magazine, for example); background features, to put the news in context; and opinion pieces (such as columns, editorials and polemical articles, designed to be provocative to the audience).

## The anatomy of a feature

While there is no fixed way to write a feature, many do share some common elements. The notion that a feature has to have a beginning, middle and end is too trite (as we shall see when considering ways of writing intros), but it is rather like a classic short story in that the reader will expect it to be coherent. While the practice of reading news means that we tend to scan stories, taking in as much detail as we consider necessary before moving to the next one, once a reader has committed to a feature story they will be much more likely to read to the end.

The simplest component of a feature, but one that should not be overlooked, is the title. An arresting title, accompanied by an eye-catching graphic, is the first thing that will make someone consider an article interesting enough to read. This is then usually followed by the standfirst, a short introduction that will include some information about the contributor(s) and give an idea of what the article is about. The following are two examples of feature titles and standfirsts:

> **Smog and Mirrors**
> Chinese officials have promised to clean up the air for the 2008 Olympics. If banishing power plants and diversity traffic doesn't work, they're willing to shut Beijing down cold. By Spencer Reiss. Photographs by Tony Law. (*Wired*)

> **Crown of the Continent**
> By Douglas H. Chadwick. Photographs by Michael Melford. By 2030, Glacier National Park may have lost all its glaciers. But with turquoise lakes, bighorn sheep, and two-mile-high peaks, Glacier-Waterton will always be a wonderland.
>
> > (*National Geographic*)

Features will nearly always list the writer (unless they are short, caption-led pieces), but not always the photographer. The fact that the two examples above do indicates just how important images are to magazine articles: virtually no one is going to read a feature that consists entirely of text.

## Structure and presentation

The presentation of a feature is extremely important for the vast majority of publications. Until the twentieth century, a magazine article looked very similar to a chapter in a book, possibly broken up by the occasional engraved image or divided into columns, but generally consisting of dense text. Innovations in photography and other areas of design, particularly typography, led to a much more experimental approach to presentation.

What should be remembered is the way that most of us read magazines: unlike a novel, where a reader starts at the beginning and works their way through in a linear fashion, most of us begin reading magazines by flicking through them from page to page.

When glancing through different features, the reader's eye is caught by pictures, boxouts, captions and other visual information that can attract him or her to read the rest of the article. And this information is *always* visual: even text is a graphic object, so short blocks of text that stand out in some way may give an insight into the feature that makes us want to read on.

Typical visual devices employed within a feature are:

- Boxes or boxouts, and panels: blocks of text that will be marked off from the main body of the article, for example, by being coloured differently to the rest of the page. These can be extremely short – giving a contact address, for example – or short, almost mini-features in their own right that convey a substantial amount of information.
- Bullet points: a simple way of drawing attention to a list of elements within an article.
- Statistical tables: writing out numerical data is the easiest way to lose a reader and makes for very tedious features, whereas the inclusion of a graph or table can get across the point of that information at a glance.
- Information graphics: increasingly popular, particularly in the B2B or more technically minded press, information graphics (such as a map of countries with data on population or diseases) is related to the charts and graphs mentioned above. It may also include such things as cutaways or technical drawings, where information is conveyed to the reader by a combination of image and captions.
- Pullquotes and captions: these are short extracts of text to illustrate an image or to make the page more visually appealing.

While a feature needs to be coherent, the comparison to a short story is misleading for a number of articles which do not follow a single narrative. It is not uncommon for magazine features to be 'broken up', to consist of a number of separate but related panels each of which provides a single focus for part of the article. For example, a health feature on a particular illness may begin with an introduction, the body copy, which outlines the condition, to be followed by a series of mini-interviews or profiles detailing sufferers and how they cope.

## Types of feature

The majority of features that appear in consumer magazines and newspaper supplements are lifestyle features: many magazines include little else and may be broken down into the following categories:

- Health and fitness: including that extremely popular staple of women's magazine, the dieting guide, one important crossover that has occurred in the past two decades is the increasing number of fitness guides into general magazines. Whereas these previously were confined to more specialist exercising magazines, a whole range of articles offering advice on exercise appear regularly elsewhere. Health articles may also deal with medical conditions and various treatments and therapies.

- Fashion and beauty: while these two are often intrinsically linked, the beauty element is also often tied to health features. A common way of attracting readers to such articles is to use an interview with a celebrity as the hook or draw for the piece.

- Leisure and hobbies: a rapidly developing sector of the lifestyle market, these titles can be very specialised, with magazines devoted entirely to one particular leisure activity. More often, such articles will cover a particular pursuit in more general titles.

- Relationships and sex: extremely popular in men's and women's titles, articles dealing with these subjects can range from the relatively innocuous, such as flirting with the opposite sex, to fairly graphic accounts of what to do in bed, or more complex articles that will focus on a psychological aspect of relationships.

- Homes and gardens: the boom in house prices in the past decade has contributed to the rise of a huge number of articles and magazines that deal with such things as home improvement tips and celebrity properties.

- Food: incorporating cooking and restaurant reviews, this is a long-established genre for general as well as specialist titles.

- Travel: travel features can consist of those that offer specific guidance on visiting places (accommodation, things to do and so on), and ones that focus more on telling a narrative about the writer's visit to a particular place or, increasingly, focusing on an aspect of the travel industry.

- Family: including the sub-category of babies and parenting, these articles will focus on relationships between family members, usually from a psychological point of view, or offer practical advice.

- The arts: in some ways a distinct category of lifestyle journalism, and a diverse one that tends to lend itself very well to reviewing, it includes articles on art, books, music, drama and film.

In addition to this general category of lifestyle features, a great many articles – particularly those that deal with celebrity or fame in some way – are based around a profile or interview. The writer is expected to conduct an in-depth interview with their subject, and for an effective article will have to engage in research before the meeting to ensure that he or she asks all the right questions, and does not simply repeat what has been published before. In addition, the profile should have an angle, a purpose that will make the audience want to read it. For example, a profile of an actor or band should be related to a new movie or album that is being released.

For the journalist conducting the interview, the craft is to convert what will almost certainly be far too much material (usually captured on tape or a digital recorder) into a compelling and coherent narrative. An article that is packed with too many quotes can actually become quite boring to read, so usually the majority of information will be reported as indirect speech, converting long quotations to single sentences and allowing more space for background information on the interviewee. Another point to bear in mind when writing such pieces is whether they are written in the first person ('X told me') or the third person, where no mention is made of the writer at all.

Another category that is a popular staple of features is the opinion or comment piece: nearly all magazines will have an editorial, whereby an editor seeks to offer his or her opinion on a subject that affects readers, but many more also include such things as gossip columns, diaries and 'op-ed' comment pieces. The talents required for such features can be varied: a gossip columnist needs to be interested in people – indeed, generally very nosy – while the opinion writer must be willing to adopt strong opinions to try to rouse the audience.

Comment pieces may merge with background or news features, particularly if investigating a subject that is potentially contentious in the spheres of business, politics, environment and so on. The point of such articles is to provide more detailed analysis of events going on in the world that will appeal to readers, and significant levels of research are needed to make such a feature authoritative and compelling.

The product round-up, also known as consumer journalism, is very common in certain types of magazine and rarely dealt with at all in others. Motoring and computer titles, for example, will often run features which compare certain types of car or PC, and the leading title in this regard is *Which?*, which regularly reviews everything from mortgages to washing machines.

Even more general lifestyle magazines may include consumer 'tests' of such things as make-up products or clothes. At the more professional end, however, a serious consumer title will have a set of standards against which a product can be tested (for example, fuel efficiency, handling and comfort for a particular car).

Such articles are avidly read by advertisers as well as consumers, and it is not uncommon for the former to try to influence the outcome of a particular test. However, any magazine that is serious about such journalism – which is becoming increasingly important in helping the reader select goods from a bewildering range of choices – will maintain strict controls over the role of manufacturers who provide goods for testing. In the US, as with *Which?* in the UK, it is not unknown for magazine editors to purchase the goods they test in order to prevent any undue influence.

## Style and content

The starting point for any feature writer is to think of the audience: although the article can (and should) be immensely creative, there is a significant difference between the creative writing associated with fiction and journalistic writing for magazines, key to which are the expectations of readers who regularly consume a particular title. An article for *The Economist* is obviously going to read very differently from one for *Heat*, and the writer must take into account the demographics and background of the audience.

Associated with this is finding the right voice. Some magazines regularly publish features written in the first voice, not necessarily that of the journalist: real-life titles, which have become very popular in recent years, for example, will offer the story of a member of the public told from their point of view, although the material is drawn from interviews and then structured into a finished article by the writer.

Similarly, opinion pieces will often offer a very forceful voice of the person writing the feature (although this itself, when it works well, is a carefully constructed version of aspects of the journalist's personality). When applied wrongly, however, such writing can seem egocentric and inappropriate, and background features, for example, work best when told from the position of an impersonal, third person narrator.

Deciding which tense to write a story in – past or present – can have a significant effect on the impact of a story. Features written in the present tense can appear much more vivid, but the danger is the temptation to slip into the past tense, which is a more natural way of presenting amounts of information about events that have been completed.

Similarly, the type of vocabulary used should be appropriate to the audience: while jargon is best avoided at all times, if you are writing a feature for a very tightly focused audience in a specific industry, say, then failing to use commonly employed terminology will make your writing seem amateurish. Even so, the long sentences and complex language associated with certain professions such as the law and academia are never appropriate outside specialised journals.

## Writing intros

With the standfirst, the intro is the hook that draws the reader into the rest of the article. Although techniques for writing intros to features are nowhere near as prescriptive as those for news stories, they should be written with the rest of the story in mind. In particular, it is important to establish the angle of your piece – whether it is a factual, news-based piece or something that draws upon 'softer' features.

Of the various types of introduction to a magazine article, commonly used ones include anecdotes or descriptions, which set the scene by describing a person or place or tell a story related to the main subject of the feature. Consider the following from a recent *Guardian Weekend* profile of Mackenzie Crook, star of the *Pirates of the Caribbean* movies and TV sitcom, *The Office*:

> 'My wife recently bought a pedometer,' Mackenzie Crook says. 'You're meant to take 10,000 steps a day, and I did 15,000 just in an average day at home. I pace all the time. I can't sit still and watch a film on TV. I have to do stuff. I'm a big twitcher. Constantly on the move.'

The point for anyone who has seen Mackenzie is that this anecdote, which has nothing to do with the ostensible purpose of the feature (a review of the actor's career at the time of the release of *Pirates of the Caribbean 3*), is immediately meant to explain his unconventional appearance. It also serves to reinforce the angle of the piece – that Mackenzie's subsequent Hollywood career has been little short of astonishing – by suggesting a deeper drive that cannot, literally, sit still.

Other techniques for opening an article include the provocative statement or question that is meant to intrigue the reader. These should make the reader think, or rouse his opinions strongly for or against the opening statement. For example, Joe Klein began one of his *Time* magazine columns during the 2004 presidential election as follows: 'Bush's argument is tight, concise and, so far, impregnable. It is also a clever distortion of reality.' Considering the divisions in the United States at the time, the beauty of such a statement was that both Republicans and Democrats would find something to disagree with.

Finally, the old stop-gap if you are really stuck for an opening is to use a quotation. Although often dismissed as lazy journalism, a carefully selected quote from your interviewee can intrigue, provoke or stimulate the reader to continue with the rest of the piece.

## The role of the features editor

The position of features editor is one of the most interesting on a magazine. For larger titles, as with the news editor, he or she will probably be responsible for a number of staff writers, and share similar responsibilities in terms of ensuring that copy is prepared for a particular section of a magazine. It is more likely, however, that the features editor will work with a number of freelance writers: the demands of deadlines tend to be looser for features and, in addition, the editor is more likely to need a wider range of expertise and experience for different types of article.

Although the tendency throughout this chapter has been to talk of a generic features editor, on many titles the need to produce longer articles tends to create not one but several editors, each with responsibility for a different type of content. Thus there may be a lifestyle editor, fashion editor, food and homes editor on a women's title, each working with different writers and freelances to produce content for the title. For all such editors, an important part of their job is to generate ideas for forthcoming issues – to do which they must keep an eye on the competition, develop expertise in their area of responsibility, and talk to industry experts as much as possible.

## Reviews

Along with news and features, reviews are a staple of many magazines, both consumer titles and B2B. A substantial proportion of titles are taken up with reviews in some shape or form, reflecting the fact that many of us buy magazines not simply to be entertained or be informed as to what is happening in the world, but also to receive advice on the bewildering array of objects and events that face us as consumers.

So, what is a review? On a very superficial level, a review tends to be longer than a news story and shorter than a feature – but this does not really define reviews. Indeed, some very effective review writing may consist of short and pithy paragraphs that convey the writer's opinion in a few lines. And this is key to a review: it must provide the writer's opinion; a critical assessment of what he or she thought of the subject under scrutiny.

A review is not simply a listing, something which conveys information about events or other topics in as neutral a fashion as possible. In addition to this, the writer has to describe what they are reviewing, whether it is a film, a meal at a restaurant or a financial service, and then offer an assessment of whether they believe it to be suitable or not.

This, in turn, raises a number of questions regarding the experience of the reviewer, which often relate to implicit opinions that he or she holds regarding the subject under review. What are the values that the reviewer uses to base judgements upon? At some level, these will come from an awareness of what else is happening in the field. For example, making the statement that something is too expensive should come from the knowledge of how much similar items are sold for elsewhere.

In a modern consumer society, reviewing provides a service. Readers are faced with immense choice, and often do not have the experience to make reasonable comparisons. This is what they look for in the reviews, and so good review writing (which is not by any means the same as a good, in the sense of favourable, review) needs to spell out what people need to know about goods and services. Ultimately, the reader will need to make up his or her own mind – and nowhere is this clearer than in matters of taste, such as film or music reviews. The cliché may be that 'everyone hates a critic', but if the critic provides an honest and thoughtful appraisal the truth is they might respect the opinion if not the person.

## The qualifications to be a reviewer

In the second act of Samuel Beckett's *Waiting for Godot*, the two principal characters Vladimir and Estragon launch into a series of insults against each other. After trading various terms of abuse such as 'moron', 'abortion', 'sewer-rat' and 'cretin', Estragon hurls the word 'Crritic' (rolled around his mouth 'with finality', we are told), causing Vladimir to visibly wilt, vanquished.

Drama has a rich tradition of insulting theatre critics, mainly because reviewers can be so damning of the plays that they see. One of the most common retorts to a bad review is to challenge the critic to put on a play. The idea is that once they realise just how difficult it is to direct and produce for the stage, they will be more sympathetic, but behind this is another assumption: that to understand a subject properly, you have to be a practitioner.

The ferocity with which theatre reviews are often rebuffed is probably due to the fact that although directing and acting require specific skills, the drama critic could potentially be seen as a failed dramatist. (Something similar occurs in literary reviewing, which is another often very vicious arena where publications such as the *London Review of Books* appear to delight in giving a book to a writer who was previously trashed in its pages by the very author of the book under review.)

In most other areas, however, such potential crossovers are rare. It is highly unlikely that the film critic will ever be able to amass the budget required to release a motion picture, and the automobile reviewer will not be employed to design cars. Yet, is there any truth in the notion that better reviews are provided by those who practise the craft they are examining? Should music reviews be written by musicians? Should we leave the appraisal of buildings to architects? And is there a role for well-written food reviews in the hands of anyone other than a top chef?

The last example may be the best one in drawing attention to what it is a reviewer does: not all of us can cook – and only a very few of us can cook exceptionally well. Yet all of us can eat, and if not everyone can eat well the task that a good reviewer sets him- or herself is often to educate the tastes (in this case literally) of the reader. And this is the most important point: the critic must write first and foremost for the reader, not the producer.

So a reviewer does not need to be a practitioner: indeed, in some areas it may be a hindrance. We want our best chefs to concentrate on their culinary skills, and while there are notable exceptions, a certain degree of verbal inadequacy is not necessarily a hindrance to producing great rock music. A reviewer, after all, is a writer, and it is in writing that his or her particular skill lies.

Despite this, the ability to produce good reviews does require a considerable amount of knowledge and expertise in a field, as well as enthusiasm for the subject. If you have no interest in film, then the chances are that your writing about the movies will be a lacklustre affair. In addition, you are hardly likely to engage with the history and background of film in such a way as to give you a solid base for comparing new releases. A reviewer does not need to *do*, but he or she does need to *understand*.

With regard to writing for the reader, another important aspect to bear in mind, as with other types of journalistic copy, is the audience for that particular magazine. Technical reviews work well when the readership of a title is technically minded, presumably because they share a similar professional background. For other markets, the reviewer will often need to provide simpler explanations, although even writing for a more specialised audience should always be clear and direct.

## Structure of a review

The first step to writing a review must be to determine your opinion of the topic under consideration – whether it is good, bad or indifferent.

In order to determine that, you must of course first note down your experience, approaching the subject with as open a mind as possible. If you have decided in advance that something is wonderful or atrocious, it is unlikely you will write a fair review (more on which later).

For busy staff writers, reviews might, unfortunately, be written on the hoof to hit imminent deadlines. Ideally, however, the reviewer should spend time preparing their piece as much as possible: a little research can go a long way. Before dealing with sense impressions, the reviewer must establish the facts, such as whether this is the first album by a band, or the price on the road of a new car.

When writing up a review, most magazines have a fairly clear format as to presentation, some elements of which will probably be quite rigid. A large number will have some form of rating system, whether stars out of five or ten or something more unusual, and it is typical to have a boxout or short section that provides a quick summary of the item and the reviewer's opinions.

For other elements of a review, the writer needs to decide where to provide such things as factual information (near the beginning, as the reader is unlikely to know much about the subject), and how much description to give before moving on to his or her verdict.

## Fair comment, libel and malicious falsehood

Expressing an opinion is the most important part of the review – and something which is often restricted by the demands of a word count, so that it can be difficult to justify your estimation as deeply as you would like. Examples should be given, not merely to avoid dull statements, but which will also indicate the writer's own taste (and allow the audience to disagree).

The issue of libel and malicious falsehood will be discussed in greater detail in Chapter 7, but it is an issue that can greatly affect review writers because so often derogatory comments will appear in print. If the reviewer truly believes that a product or service is poor, then he or she must say so – but no critic is immune to libel laws.

This situation became even more pointed in 2007 with two libel cases for food reviews. The first, successfully brought by Goodfellas restaurant against *The Irish News*, saw the paper have to pay £25,000 plus costs for what was described by the plaintiff as a 'hatchet job'. The second, in Philadelphia, was initiated by a three-line review by Craig LaBan in the *Philadelphia Inquirer* that dismissed a meal as 'expensive and disappointing'. There has been a long string of suits brought against food critics in the US, some of which were successful at the original trial only to be overturned on appeal on the basis of protecting freedom of expression.

In the UK as well, the right to publish an honest opinion – under what is known as 'fair comment' – means that a reviewer has the right to be as unfair as he or she likes as long as this is their true opinion. However, getting facts wrong (even if this is an 'honest' mistake) is no defence, and if opinion is seen as over the top or maliciously motivated, this too can lead to a libel prosecution.

At the other end of the scale, the fear of libel, as well as a sometimes pernicious influence of advertisers in publications that fear losing out on any advertising, can result in bland and boring reviews. It is probably going a little too far to describe it as the reviewer's *duty* to publish his or her honest opinion, but if the alternative is dull and tedious copy it is certainly a service to the reader to write what they think.

## The role of the reviews editor

The reviews editor, when employed on a sizable title, will have similar responsibilities in many respects to the news and features editor, having to manage a team and provide ideas for forthcoming issues.

Something that can be substantially different, especially for those magazines in which reviews of goods play an important role, is that the editor will also need to organise some way of dealing with incoming items. Many magazines are sent lots of items for review, and the editor will have to put in place a system for getting these to freelances or staff writers, and ensuring that expensive goods are returned to the appropriate manufacturer.

For some titles that deal with particularly complicated items, such as computers or electronic goods, there may even need to be some sort of 'lab'. In many cases, this could simply be part of a room set aside to test equipment, but alongside it there will be some sort of set of tests that will provide for equal treatment of products from different producers.

## Commissioning

While commissioning freelance writers is sometimes treated as a black art, the essentials are generally straightforward: commissioning editors (usually a section editor) will have to negotiate with a writer within the constraints of an editorial budget. The amount available will probably vary from month to month, as some magazines have different amounts of editorial in different issues, but the commissioning editor will need to know what is available to him or her.

The next step is to determine levels of payment: typically, freelances are paid per 1,000 words, and for some titles there will be a fixed fee, but others will vary the amounts paid depending on whether they wish to attract certain, more experienced writers. Yet others will always require some degree of negotiation or, say when hiring freelances to cover an important event for which no staff writers are available, a day fee, including expenses.

### Writing a brief

When a commissioning editor has located suitable writers, and before any negotiations take place, he or she will need to provide them with a brief. As the name suggests, this should be concise but also comprehensive, outlining what the editor expects the freelance to do, including any angle to be taken, specific content that may be required and additional features to be included in the article such as boxouts or panels. For some titles, the writer may also be required to provide pictures or graphics.

The brief will also need to include a deadline, which is not the deadline for publication but, rather, when copy needs to be returned to the magazine so that it can be subbed and laid out appropriately. Writers will almost certainly wish to know, however, when a piece will appear, particularly if payment is to be made 30 days after publication. In addition, some articles will require a very specific word count to fill a particular space, while others will be the average required for a certain number of pages: if the writer over-writes, the fee remains the same.

The final question to be determined (after delivery – usually email these days, at least for copy) is rights. Copyright will be discussed more fully in Chapter 7, but one thing to bear in mind when commissioning is the distinction between First British Serial Rights, the right to publish once in a British newspaper or magazine, and full rights for redistribution internationally or via another medium such as the web. Typically, publishers will ask for a writer to 'assign', or sell, the copyright, or will demand an unlimited licence to redistribute the writer's copyrighted work in different media.

In the second half of the 1990s, particularly as the Internet was becoming an ever more popular medium, this approach caused considerable consternation among freelances. In practice, very little written work (as opposed to images, where it still remains contentious) is re-sold, but an editor may need to exercise sensitivity, particularly when dealing with a famous or well-established writer.

Sometimes, the commission may still be sent out as a letter – it is, after all, a contract between publisher and writer, which the latter must sign and send back. More often, however, details will be sent in an email, with a corresponding reply serving as confirmation.

## Rewrites and kill fees

Sometimes an article will be unusable, sometimes because of a fault on the part of the magazine (for example, pages have been cut because not enough ads have been sold), but more often than not because the writer has not produced what the editor expected. Strictly speaking, a kill fee is payment made to close a contract before the commission is completed, but more usually it is made after copy comes in and it cannot be used in the title.

Obviously, if the work is completely unprofessional then the writer can be seen to have failed to fulfil his part of the contract and so does not deserve payment (although obviously the writer may see things very differently). More often, although there are problems with a piece the writer may still be useful for future work. In these cases, a kill fee is the most suitable way to close the commission. These should be used sparingly, however: not only are they simply a waste of money that could be better spent elsewhere, but such payments are likely to sour relations in some way between the magazine and the freelance.

Alternatively, if a piece can be salvaged, it is perfectly reasonable to ask for a rewrite under the terms of the original commission. If the article is still to appear in the same issue of the magazine, obviously the turn-around for such a piece will be very tight. In addition, the editor is then committed to paying a full fee even if the piece is not used – in which case it may be simpler to pay a kill fee and have it rewritten in-house.

Finally, when sent a piece 'on spec', the editor must make it very clear that this is simply being considered – it has not been commissioned and so, if it is not used, no fee is paid.

## Freelances versus staff writers

The issues around rights draw attention to one distinction between using freelance writers and in-house staff: under British law, staff writers have no copyright over their own material, so copy produced in such a way can be re-used as the editor sees fit. Indeed, the potential for conflict that emerged in the 1990s did see a movement away from relying on small numbers of staff and a larger stable of freelances, although this has become much less of an issue in recent years.

There are, however, other times when it is better to use staff writers. Some articles (and news stories feature very highly in this way) require a considerable amount of work and research to produce a small amount of copy. Staff writers can pursue such things as phone calls from the office as they do other tasks during the day.

Likewise, if an editor wishes to try a new type of feature, which may or may not end up being used in a magazine, it is better to use somebody already employed by the title than potentially waste money commissioning a freelance. Similarly, if a project is particularly sensitive, in most cases a staff journalist should be employed so that competitors do not know what is being planned.

Yet no substantial magazine will rely entirely on staffers: for variety in terms of writing, as well as the need to call on different levels of expertise, all editors will seek to maintain a contact list of freelances that they can call on to provide copy.

## Subbing

For many students working on a magazine project for the last time, the temptation is to view layout as the last stage of the production cycle, with sub-editing viewed as a necessary evil that can be skipped over as quickly as possible. Yet subbing is a valuable skill that is essential to professional magazine production, so valuable in fact that editors often have a harder time recruiting suitable sub-editors than they do getting decent journalists to fill a staff-writing role.

At its most basic level, sub-editing involves quality control, looking for factual errors, typos or literals and solecisms to ensure that everything is accurate and well-written. As well as this, the sub-editor plays an important role in the production cycle by ensuring that copy fits both in terms of its layout on the page and with a house style. For many titles subs also have the job of thinking up titles and standfirsts for articles (although on others this is an editor's task), and nearly all will expect them to provide such things as captions for images.

When dealing with copy, the first thing that a sub must do is focus on clarity to make sure the article is readable for the magazine audience. While journalists may be very close to their sources, often adding too much detail and even writing in jargon, subs will often wish to simplify and explain – although plain English is not the same as dull language. It is for this reason that subbing always has to be done by another person: while a writer can check his or her own copy for mistakes, what they have written will nearly always be meaningful to them. For the sub, however, this will be the first encounter with copy that, if it is not clear, may need changing.

Regarding inaccuracies, these fall into two types. First of all there are mistakes of spelling, grammar and syntax. The second type consists of factual errors, which might need to be rectified by a phone call or checking another source. Too many of the former make a publication appear unprofessional to the reader; the latter might go unnoticed by most readers but can have more serious consequences, especially if they lead to inadvertently libellous statements. Potentially contentious statements should be referred to an editor.

Such activities, while important, do not themselves make substantial changes to the text. However, when dealing with an art department that will provide a layout, the sub-editor's job also consists of making copy fit the page, and in some cases this can involve considerable adjustments. Text may need to be cut or even expanded, and if these are more than minor, an editor, and probably the author, should be informed (and asked to rewrite): this is one area where a sub can inadvertently introduce his or her own mistakes. In addition, captions, pull-quotes and other additional visual elements need to be added.

Where other changes may take place is with regard to the house style. Any magazine that uses a range of writers will have a variety of voices – as, indeed, it should – to prevent articles becoming too monotonous. However, some degree of uniformity should be imposed across a magazine. In some cases, this will be minor issues of style, such as whether to use digits or words for small numbers (6 as opposed to six), or terms of address when required. In other cases, there may be certain ways that a magazine likes to refer to topics that are regularly covered, or it may have a style that is informal or formal for various subjects.

# 5
# Photography and design

While the verbal content that goes into an article is extremely important, providing the matter that will entertain and inform readers for the
hours that they choose to read a magazine, the visual content cannot
and should not be considered at all inferior. Since the invention of
photography, and the revolutions in design and print technologies that
occurred in the early twentieth century and again, after the Second World
War, the way magazines *look* has become essential to their appeal to
readers.

Throughout the last century, magazines have evolved to be an almost
perfect medium for photography in particular, and since the 1970s and
1980s certainly most consumer publications have moved to glossy
production values which show off visuals to the best effect. Good magazine
design is a combination of illustration, typography and colour, all of
which must be joined together into an effective layout. The first three
elements are the subject of this chapter, and we shall consider principles
of design layout in the next.

## Impact versus beauty

Most designers will probably wish to produce a magazine that is a beautiful
aesthetic object – but beauty is very much in the eye of the beholder
and a subjective value that does not always work best towards particular
designs. As Morrish (2003) observes, for many titles beauty is a far too
static ideal and what a good designer works towards is *impact*.

This can be very evident in some of the best-selling titles in the UK,
European and American markets, some of which look garish by any
standards. Notions such as harmonising colours or selecting subtle images

and logos appear to have been discarded, to be replaced by bright, neon lettering on brash, day-glo colours. And yet the designs of these magazines work – battling it out on the front line of the newsstand to attract notoriously promiscuous readers who flit from title to title each week.

Of course, when chasing a mass market, the design techniques for such titles have to be loud and rather kitsch. But titles that do not seek such wide circulation will obviously wish to announce very different values in terms of design. Using more restrained colours and balanced designs, titles such as *Vogue* and *Wallpaper\** wish to indicate to both advertisers and readers that they are much classier than the tabloids. One publisher I knew would regularly read *Cigar Afficionado*: he did not smoke, and thus had little interest in cigars themselves, but the lush advertising and understated articles on the finer things of life appealed to the rich life-style he wished to lead (or, equally importantly, wished others to believe he led).

## The role of the art editor

The art editor's role is vital to the success of the magazine – indeed, alongside that of the publisher and the editor is probably the most important to how it is received in the market. Because the visual impact will affect readers so immediately, this can have a great effect on circulation, so the art editor and editor will need to work in close conjunction.

As well as coming up with ideas for design and illustration him- or herself, the art editor will be responsible for a team of layout artists and designers if working for a sizeable publication. The role is also one of the most significant in terms of commissioning: the art editor has to build up a stable of freelances who can provide photography and illustration, and while some of this can probably be done in-house the chances are that it will come from external sources.

For some titles where famous or proprietary images have to be sourced on a regular basis, there may be a separate picture editor, but on most titles this will be another responsibility of the art editor, or one which he or she delegates to a member of the design team.

As well as being expected to provide a coherent design for the entire magazine, the single most important page that the art editor has to take responsibility for is the cover, as this is what will attract or turn off readers at the newsstand. As part of the job, he or she will have to think up new ideas – working alongside the editor and production department (who typically think up the cover lines) to ensure that this has the greatest possible impact.

The tendency of most consumer magazines today has, rather depressingly, been to rely on a single photograph of an individual. While some of these can still have a remarkable effect (and seem to be expected by most readers), it does mean that there is less space than ever before for expressing abstract ideas through the cover. Obviously there are exceptions – such as computer and car magazines, although even these tend to rely on stock images of the products they cover. Ironically, it is probably in some sectors of the B2B press that the most imaginative approach has been taken to presenting abstract cover ideas in recent years.

In addition to managing the in-house studio and dealing with freelances, the final managerial task of the art editor is to work with external agencies that will provide some elements of printing and colour work. While much of this will fall into the remit of the production editor, dealt with in the next chapter, this can take up a substantial amount of the art editor's time and budget.

## Working with designers

In the vast majority of cases, layout (dealt with in much more detail in the next chapter) will typically be done in-house. This makes most sense as pages need to be modified or amended on a day-by-day basis, and all but the smallest editorial team will have graphic designers either dedicated to their magazine, or part of a centralised art team. Very small magazines might commission a designer to provide a template which is then filled in with copy and photos by the editor or an editorial assistant.

For photography and illustration, while some elements of these will be done in-house it is more likely that much of the work will be done by freelances. As with written features, composing an accompanying illustration for an article can be too time-consuming for layout artists who have to get pages ready for print.

Similarly with photography, not only can a photo shoot be quite protracted, but a professional photographer will fulfil all the requirements for studio and equipment. In addition, while photographs make up a huge proportion of the content of most magazines it is usually only for short periods of time during the production cycle that the editor needs to concentrate on photography. It is much more sensible to hire freelances, or for multi-title companies to hire photographers who work across several magazines.

On some titles, for example, those that deal with celebrity, the freelance has become essential in his or her most notorious form: as a member of the paparazzi. Elsewhere, the number of freelance photographers employed by magazines simply draws attention to the fact that no staff member can hope to be in every place all of the time.

This is a situation that is very different to the regional (if not national) press. For a long time it had been the custom on local newspapers to employ one or more photographers who would go out with reporters to take pictures for the daily paper. With tight deadlines, this made sense. Increasingly, however, at least for smaller offices, reporters themselves are expected to take a digital camera with them. On newsprint, an editor can get away with this (particularly as the photos were always unlikely to be of studio quality anyway); the visual impact of glossies means that there are no chances of this happening in the vast majority of magazines.

## Elements of magazine design

For the rest of this chapter, we will consider the various elements that go into magazine design before concentrating on bringing them together in a page layout in the next chapter.

## Text and typography

So far, this book has dealt with the style and content of text from the point of view of writers and editors, but, as has already been mentioned, text also functions in a magazine as part of the design. Columns and blocks of text, combined with such things as boxes and pull-quotes, create a dynamic design that will draw the eye into the page as the reader moves from small, concentrated snippets of information such as a picture caption into the main body of the article.

What is more, in all but the dullest of magazine designs, text has to work in conjunction with other graphic elements, particularly photographs or illustrations and also colour on the page.

## Fonts and typefaces

Although the terms font and typeface are often used interchangeably, a typeface was traditionally a complete set of characters in multiple fonts and sizes, while a font was a typeface in one size and style, such as italic or bold. It is common usage today to employ font (or, more rarely, fount) to mean typeface, and that is how the word will be used throughout the rest of this chapter.

As well as italic and bold, font styles also include Roman (the standard, or default, script for word processors), bold italic, condensed, extended, and small capitals. There are several others, but these are the ones most commonly used in print. In the UK and US, type size is measured in points, with approximately 72 points to the inch. Another method, used in mainland Europe, is the didot system, where type is measured in ciceros.

One thing to bear in mind is that while there is a wide range of point sizes familiar to any user of a word processor, typically 8 to 72, the actual print sizes of different fonts are not exactly the same (which is why, for example, 10 point Arial looks bigger than 10 point Times New Roman).

Obviously, font size has an important part to play in page design, with larger text catching the reader's eye more quickly than small text, and setting different parts of the page in different type sizes will build up its own logic of how to read the page. A headline in a large font will be read first, and small captions or text at the end of the article indicates to the reader that he or she does not need to look at this to understand the content on the page.

At the same time, font styles will also change the way the reader approaches the page. Captions, for example, will typically be in a smaller font size than body text, yet by placing them in bold the reader's eye will be drawn to them more quickly. Similarly, use of italics is the most common way to emphasise text, but sometimes the use of a different face such as SMALL CAPS can have a more dramatic impact.

## Legibility and experimentation

While there is much more that can be written on the use of typography (with Frost's *Designing for Newspapers and Magazines* providing a good introduction to this subject), here we shall limit ourselves to just a couple more pointers that should be considered by anyone designing a magazine page.

The first point is that modern computer programs such as QuarkXPress and Adobe InDesign provide access to a potentially bewildering array of different typefaces such as Baskerville Old Face and Monotype Corsica. Students experimenting for the first time with typography are often tempted to try out as many of these fonts as possible, but there is a very good reason why most print is restricted to a handful of faces: legibility.

In contrast to posters and covers, where there is plenty of room for experimentation, the majority of magazines still consist of large sections of print, and attempting to read anything over an extended period of time in a kooky typeface becomes a chore for the reader. Even worse is the tendency to mix a large number of typefaces on a page – a particularly heinous crime if it is done within body text. At best, a designer will restrict him or herself to three or four different typefaces to clearly mark out separate design elements, such as headings, subheadings, captions and body text.

---

**An example of a sans serif font, Gill Sans MT**

**This is Gill Sans MT Condensed at the same point size**

An example of a serif font, Garamond

*This is Garamond italic at the same point size*

---

**Figure 5.1** Sans serif and serif fonts

The second point is the distinction between serif and sans serif fonts. When writing with quills, letters formed thick and thin strokes, which remain in many modern fonts as little curlicues on the end of each letter. Sans serif fonts do not have these small flourishes, and became popular in the twentieth century as a more 'modern' typeface design. In practice, serif fonts seem to be preferred by most readers as more legible and so used for large sections of body text, with sans serif used for headings and covers because individual letters stand out more clearly.

## Fonts and print

When using fonts in certain programs, particularly earlier versions of QuarkXPress, it should always be borne in mind that there may be issues of compatibility between one computer system (that used by the publisher) and another (that used by the printer). While the move to PDF and embedding fonts (see the next chapter) means that this is much less of a problem than previously, in some cases it is still necessary to provide any unusual fonts that may be used in a design on disk to a printer. Without this, the program may revert to a default font (such as Helvetica or Times) that ruins the page design.

There are different font technologies used for screen displays and print, but the most common ones are TrueType, Postscript Type 1 and OpenType. Postscript Type 1 is the older digital format, devised by Adobe in 1985 and still commonly used. These fonts contain only some information embedded in the font itself, while the rest must be handled by Adobe Type Manager (included with most Adobe programs or part of MacOS X). This often distinguishes between a screen font, displayed on the computer monitor, and a print font which is actually handled by a compatible printer.

TrueType, designed by Apple and Microsoft in 1990, includes all information about the font in the font file itself. Postscript is still very popular for commercial printing because Adobe software has become so popular and is built into high-end printers, but there is less scope for error when printing with TrueType.

OpenType, developed more recently by Adobe in conjunction with Microsoft, works on the TrueType format but also includes Postscript information that can extend the character set (to include more letters beyond the usual limits of the font) and advanced typographic controls.

## Leading, kerning and justification

As well as type size, the presentation of text on a page is affected by leading (pronounced 'ledding') and kerning, essentially the space between lines and between letters.

Leading, which takes its name from the strips of lead that were used by printers to separate rows of type, is the white space between lines of text. Setting the same font size in different leading sizes can have an impact on how we read a page. Setting font size and leading size to the same amount usually makes text look too cramped, while increasing the latter by as little as two points (say 12 point leading for a 10 point font) can dramatically improve legibility. Increasing leading even more can give a light, airy feel to a page – very useful if that is the impression you wish to convey, less so if you want your page to look busy.

Kerning refers to the process of adjusting the space between letters. Just as individual letters can vary in vertical size, with ascenders and descenders

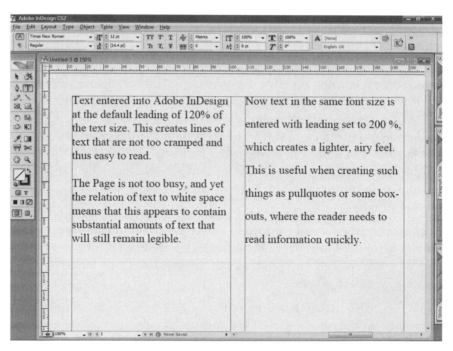

**Figure 5.2** Examples of different amounts of text leading

helping to distinguish letters such as 'b' and 'p', so the width of letters such as 'l' and 'w' can be very different. A monotype font, such as Courier, gives exactly the same amount of space to each letter, and looks less appealing aesthetically than kerned fonts, which increase or decrease the space between letters.

Kerning is largely handled automatically by modern software, but occasionally – particularly when designing a cover – the art editor may wish to make manual changes. This is because certain combinations of letters can look slightly odd, with a little too much or too little white space between them.

Justification refers to the alignment of text, with fully justified text being aligned on both the left- and right-hand sides of the page or column. Usually in magazines and newspapers, text is only justified on the left and allowed to run 'ragged right', with lines being uneven on the right-hand side of the column. In contrast to most books, where text is nearly always fully justified, leaving one side ragged improves legibility in body copy arranged in columns.

## Text presentation

When arranging text graphically on the page, there are several devices that can be used to make it more visually appealing before even considering such things as illustrations or colour.

When dealing with statistical information, or a series of lists, text is much easier to read when tabulated (arranged into a table). The eye moves easily from one column to the next and the reader can take in at a glance data that would be confusing when presented in the form of sentences.

Drop letters or drop caps are large initial letters at the beginning of an article or section heading. These can be a very simple way to draw the reader's attention to where they should start reading, or to indicate a break in the body copy. Visually, as well, they add interest and flair to a page when used judiciously.

Subheadings, or crossheads, or short lines of text between certain paragraphs, again provide visual interest to an article. They are also useful to the reader (and often the writer) in helping to structure a piece:

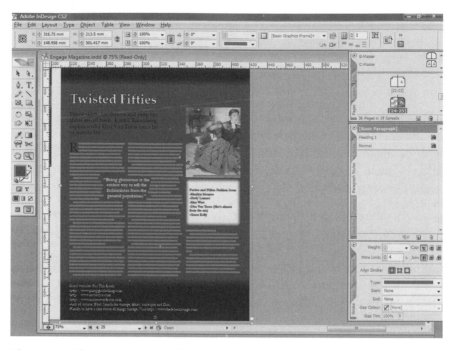

**Figure 5.3** Elements such as boxouts and captions help text stand out

occasional subheadings help to indicate a change in topic in the article, where the writer is moving in a new direction, and so serve as signposts to orient the reader.

As discussed in the previous chapter, boxed text and panels help to distinguish information and are incredibly important to a lot of magazine design. Alongside bullet points and indented text, these are some of the most common ways to lay out body copy so that it is not too uniform and dull.

For all these devices and other font styles (such as the use of bold or italics), the important point is that body copy, the substantial portion of text in the article, stands as the baseline from which text can be organised visually. There should be uniformity across body copy in a magazine – not simply on the page, but also between articles – that emphasises professional design.

Too much uniformity, however, makes a publication look dull. The use of different font styles for such things as headings, subheadings and standfirsts, as well as textual devices such as boxouts, drop letters and tables, creates a dynamic rather than static design. When reading a novel, we will concentrate on a narrative for an extended period of time, but this is not how we read a magazine: instead, our eyes move about the pages, taking in snippets of information before returning to concentrate on the articles that appear to be of most interest.

## Colour

Like typography, colour is another subject that could easily be dealt with in an entire book and will only be dealt with here fairly briefly in terms of preparing the reader to start thinking of design.

Today there are very few national magazines that are not printed in full colour throughout, although this is a relatively recent phenomenon having only really become predominant since the rise of the glossies in the 1970s. And yet the impact of colour is so important, drawing the reader into the page, that we tend to consider magazines printed in monochrome as being less vivid. Certainly advertisers do not like black and white, which is one reason why so many magazines are printed in colour.

Ironically, because colour print is so prevalent in the magazine world, there are times when use of monochrome can have a significant effect: black and white, as many photographers know, often picks up gradations of tone much more effectively than colour and so is used to give an 'arty' appeal to some features. However, while this can have an appeal when used sparingly, no commercial title would willingly revert to monochrome for all its pages.

Alternatively, publications that wish to emphasise their more radical credentials, or their independence from advertisers, may willingly embrace black and white to give themselves a feel that is closer to a fanzine or underground publication. In general, though, those magazines that are printed in monochrome tend to be very small affairs with limited budgets for design.

## Colour perception

Colour is perceived in the eye via cells called cones that distinguish different combinations of red, green and blue. Light is part of the electromagnetic spectrum, with different wavelengths being seen by the eye as different colours: longer waves in the spectrum are perceived as red, with shorter waves seen as blue.

This leads to two very different ways of presenting colour for the designer: the first is via a computer screen, where pixels display the primary hues red, green or blue light, mixing them with surrounding pixels to create any of a potential 16.7 million colours. This creates what is known as the RGB (red, green, blue) model of colour perception, and mixing all the primary colours together equally gives white light.

Print, however, works by colour *reflection*. Some of the wavelengths in a spectrum are absorbed when they hit a surface, while others are reflected back. In print, the combination of colours works best when the secondary, rather than primary, hues are mixed – that is cyan, magenta and yellow (CMY). These are the hues for inks (as opposed to paints) that are obtained when blue and green are mixed to give cyan, red and blue are mixed to give magenta, and red and green are mixed to give yellow.

Mixing all colours equally should give black, but in practice this tends to result in a muddy, brownish colour. For this reason, black is added to the mix to give what is referred to as the CMYK ('K' from blacK) model of colour perception.

In addition to mixing inks, colour is affected by another range of values known as hue, saturation and value. Hue refers to the colour itself, and saturation is the amount of that hue present on the page (for example, a darker or lighter red): 100 per cent is complete colour, 0 per cent no colour (in print, this is grey rather than white). Value represents the relative brightness of a colour: at 100 per cent it becomes white, at 0 it becomes black.

## Colour separation

Because of the way colour works on the page, by absorbing certain wavelengths and reflecting others, print has evolved over the past two centuries in particular to enable colours to be represented as accurately as possible.

When an image is imported into a computer program, either through scanning or from a digital camera, it will appear on the screen in an

RGB format, that is each shade of colour is formed by merging the hues red, green and blue. However, as we have already seen, this is no good for print, which is why certain programs such as Adobe Photoshop allow you to separate out the colours and convert them to a format suitable for printing.

Colour separation works out the colour channels for cyan, magenta, yellow and black (and an advanced image editor such as Photoshop allows you to view each of these channels separately). This results in four separate images, each of which can be fed through a different coloured part of the press to build up a full-colour picture.

Ink is transparent, and the process of printing with ink has often been called 'mixing light', in that unlike pigments such as paint it is still possible to see the colour underneath, whereas paint covers all the layers beneath it. In practice, the yellow plate is printed first, and to this is added cyan (which when mixed with different amounts of yellow produces greens) and then red to build up all other colours. Where there is no ink on the page, the paper will show through as white, and black is added finally to emphasise dark shades or for text.

The CMYK system of printing is also known as process colour. For designers, this can create problems in that colours as they appear on screen may be subtly different to those in print, and colour calibration of monitors can be quite a time-consuming process. Even then, an art editor never completely knows how a colour will appear on the page until it is printed, hence the development of such things as 'cromies', or colour proofs, that will be discussed in the next chapter.

Another colour system that has been devised is the Pantone colour system – a system of shades whereby every colour is given a number that corresponds to a certain hue, saturation and value. By entering a Pantone number, the print system picks the exact colour from an internationally agreed set of hues – although there will always be slight vagaries from magazine to magazine due to such things as variances in paper quality.

## Colour management and monitor calibration

How the eye perceives colour can make it difficult to be sure that we are seeing the exact colour that we want to see, particularly when moving between a monitor and print. Even in daily life, however, different lighting conditions and subtle differences between shades mean that we may not entirely know what colour we are looking at – for example, if the red of an old Routemaster bus is the same as the red of a post box.

When working digitally, certain colours are ascribed absolute values based on a mixture of red, green and blue pixels, each of which is set between 0 and 255. Pure red, for example, consists of a red value of 255 and 0 each for green and blue. However, taking two different monitors and setting colours to 255, 0, 0, will result in different hues on the screen. The red here is said to be 'device dependent', and the problem only becomes worse when transferred to print which normally does not even include pure red in the mix.

Colour management is the process whereby the different reds displayed by different devices (monitors and printers) are linked to consistent standards to make them useful. To do this typically requires the use of ICC profiles – ICC standing for the Independent Colour Consortium, an organisation that sets a series of standards for known colour values, or Lab Colour.

Lab Colour theoretically describes all the colours the human eye can see (actually, many more), and for accurate work a monitor and printer have to be matched to the known colour values for different hues. To calibrate a monitor for colour management, a colour-sensitive instrument is hung from the screen and the software provided with it flashes known colours against it. This creates a profile of the monitor that can be recorded and imported into programs such as Photoshop to adjust settings when working with colour.

A similar process has to be carried out on a printer: a colour test chart is printed out and then it is scanned using a spectrophotometer, a special device that can create a profile of the individual printer and adjust its settings in software for accurate colour representation. For professional printing, the calibration of the printing press is not carried out by the publisher, but ICC profiles for registered devices can be imported into computers used by a magazine to ensure as accurate as possible comparisons between the screen and the page.

Of course, the art department will need to calibrate their own monitors. In addition, screens have to be adjusted for brightness and contrast, a process known as gamma correction, to ensure that black and white appear as perfectly as possible, with no hint of colour and proper distinctions between shades of grey.

## Colour and text

Colour is one of the most vivid ways for a page to create impact. Most books on colour theory will emphasise the importance of harmonising colours, but as has already been seen when discussing aesthetic values and impact, canny publishers will often sacrifice the former for the latter. Colour clashes that would be viewed with horror in other fields are often splashed garishly across covers and spreads of magazines that delight in a certain trashy appeal: they are getting the readers, and this is not a failure of aesthetic judgement but a triumph of commercial sense.

However, when providing some guidance to potential magazine designers who want to know the proscribed artistic rules before they tear them up to pursue the strategy that works for their title, it is best to understand that generally colour is more appealing when it is in harmony with the rest of the page.

In practice, this tends to mean no more than three main shades across a page, and the use of certain colours that do not clash or produce un-wanted visual effects (such as red and blue placed side by side). For text, this also means that, in nearly every single case, the most legible type for most readers is black on white. For some dyslexics, especially those suffering from scotopic sensitivity (where the eye reacts unusually to colour), black on white results in colour aberrations where text appears to jump around on screen, but testing of other readers suggests that we take in words more easily when there is most contrast between dark print and the page.

Large sections of different coloured text, then, will be hard to read. How-ever, the astute use of small coloured text elements, such as subheadings, titles and pull-quotes, will add considerably to the page and help these jump out from the main body copy.

## Trapping and knockout

Different colours on a page may sometimes misalign when printed, resulting in ugly white spaces on the page or overlapping inks – that is the colours (printed on separate plates) are not correctly registered (or aligned). One way to avoid this problem is to design pages so that blocks of different colours do not touch, which avoids the need for trapping. Alternatively, it is possible to print black on top of two closely touching colours which will (in most cases, but not always) hide any misalignments that may take place.

Trapping refers to the process of dealing with closely registered plates where inks will touch or overlap. It is actually a series of techniques for handling colours.

The first is known as choke or spread: it involves extending the area of a lighter colour so that when the darker ink is applied there will be no white areas left if the plates shift slightly. The lighter ink overlaps the area covered by the darker one. This is called spreading if a light area is surrounded by dark, choking if the area covered is the other way around.

Knockout is another stage in printing that often requires trapping: this refers to the fact that when two different blocks of colour are printed so that they apparently overlap, say a dark blue circle over a yellow circle, what is actually printed is a dark blue circle and a yellow crescent. The area of yellow that cannot be seen is knocked out. However, if the

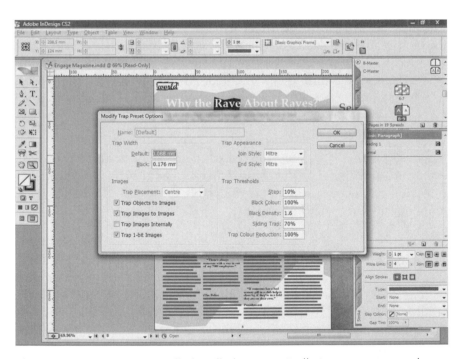

**Figure 5.4** Trapping is usually handled automatically in a program such as InDesign

plates are not correctly registered, a white gap can appear so the yellow needs to be slightly extended to ensure no white gap appears.

Trapping is usually applied automatically in DTP software such as QuarkXPress or InDesign.

## Psychology and symbolism

Colour has an important psychological and cultural effect on us, so that we have learnt to associate certain values with different colours. Blue, for example, is typically seen as calming, red as either warming or aggressive depending on its context.

Whether these responses to colour are 'hard-wired' as it were into our psyches or more the result of cultural and social values is beyond the scope of this book. Art editors should probably beware of relying too much on the former, however, particularly if they have to work for an international audience. In Japan, for example, the same word is used to denote green and blue, and while white is a colour associated with marriage in the west, for Japanese people it is the colour worn to funerals.

This brings us on to the clearly social elements of colour, where they fulfil a particular symbolism such as indicating rank or political affiliation. Some colours may be used in different cultures to indicate a particular festival or year, and so articles dealing with these topics may subtly reinforce an approach or angle by using related hues.

## Branding

While colour symbolism is important within a magazine for certain associations, such as red, white and blue for a story on the US or Union Jack, colour can also have an added significance for magazines in terms of branding. Advertisers have for a long time worked on building up certain associations between colours and products, for example, orange with a mobile phone company of the same name, or red and Coca-Cola. Colour branding often developed as a way to circumvent other advertising restrictions for particular goods, so that the manufacturers of Silk Cut cigarettes hoped that when anyone saw a particular shade of purple, they would immediately think of their cigarettes.

Such branding associations are often employed by magazine designers to promote their title. It is rare for branding to work by colour alone – there are simply too many magazines with red somewhere in the title for this to work – but in combination with a particular logo or typeface colour is an effective tool in creating a brand.

## Photography

Ever since it was introduced in the early twentieth century, photography has become an essential ingredient in what we expect from magazines. Indeed, throughout the last hundred years it is in magazine titles that the most innovative and experimental designs combining word and image have often appeared.

While the considerations of what makes a good photo are beyond the scope of this title, the importance of photography and how to use an image are essential to magazine production.

Larger magazines will employ photographers (either working solely for that title or employed by a publishing company to work across multiple titles), but many rely on freelances. The other sources for photos are picture libraries and PR companies. The latter can be useful for such things as studio shots of individuals or products that may be covered by the magazine, but they will also seek to pressurise an editor to include rather dull images of a particular person or item that they wish to promote – and which may not be part of a good story.

When using photography, being dull is probably one of the worst charges that can be laid against an image. Indeed, for many magazines, varying photographs with other forms of illustration is a good way to prevent pages looking too uniform. Photos themselves should be used to illustrate quickly what an article is about. This may emphasise any emotional impact that emerges from a story, or allow the reader to identify with any people who feature in it. On a more mundane level, they may simply identify what is being discussed, although articles that rely on a product shot or portrait as the main illustration run the danger of providing rather boring layouts.

Unlike newspaper photography, however, the sheer variety of magazines means that it can be difficult to make overall suggestions that will fit every type of publication. What is important is to understand the audience:

the rather graphic and extreme images that appear in *Bizarre* magazine, for example, will never go down well with the readers of *Homes and Gardens*.

This said, the importance of illustration and making a point cannot be underestimated. If readers can see a scene or item – for example, a new building or a car – it will help them understand the significance of an article in a way that verbal description alone simply cannot achieve.

Beyond this, photographs set the emotional response to a feature and, it must be said, they have learnt a great deal in this regard from advertising. While this may not be considered such a good thing by those used to working on newspapers or cultural critics of the magazine industry, the appeal of the glossies is precisely because they embody many of the desires and aspirations of their readers in a vivid format.

## Types of photograph

The kinds of images that tend to appear in magazines largely fall into one of a number of categories: portraits, action shots, scenes, or product shots.

Portraits, which may be head shots or full-length images of a subject, are a staple of nearly every type of magazine, and serve a number of important functions. The most obvious is that they immediately identify the subject being written about: if we have a photograph of a mountain climber or movie star, then we know who is under discussion and will recognise that person if they are a celebrity. For all photographs commissioned by a magazine, the photographer will need to get the subject to sign a model-release form, allowing the image to be used in the publication.

The issue of celebrity raises another feature regarding the use of such images. Glamorous shots of famous people have long been a way of enabling (or, depending on your point of view, seducing) readers to identify with particular desires and aspirations and have often been used by advertisers to sell products and editors to sell magazines. More recently, celebrity photography in titles such as *Heat* has tended not towards the sycophantic but rather towards the gossipy and bitchy, taking a lead from tabloid newspapers to use paparazzi photos that portray individuals in a less than glamorous light.

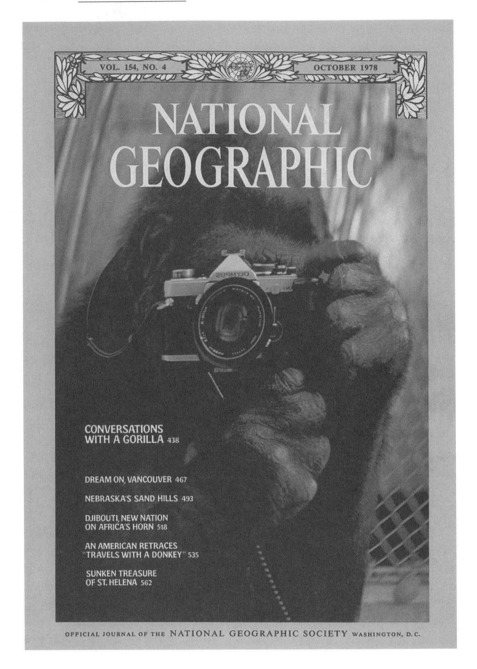

**Figure 5.5** Magazines such as *National Geographic* are rightly famous for their photography. Photo by Koko the gorilla. Used with kind permission from Dr Ronald Cohn.

While faces and bodies sell – sometimes to the dismay of critics who lay much of the blame for the dissatisfaction that many females feel around their own bodies at the door of magazine editors – the preponderance of portraits means that they have lost their impact. Scenes offer great scope to an art designer: a dramatic landscape, or lovingly arranged home interior, can provide a stunning backdrop to a feature that will draw in the reader's attention. A title such as *National Geographic* has become famous for the quality of photographs that it uses to present the world around us. And this is an important point about such images: they are not merely decoration but often provide useful information that cannot be conveyed by words alone. Even B2B titles may find that photographs of a factory or industrial setting can immediately present the reader with a sense of what is going on in a story.

The images that are most fun to do, but also the most difficult to achieve, are action shots. Sport titles, for example, require images that capture a game during the thick of things to give an impression of what happened and the atmosphere of a sporting event. Many other titles, such as automobile magazines, will try to add some drama to their images by conveying speed and movement in a single image rather than a static shot.

Which leads finally onto product photography: often under-rated, there is a real skill to creating vibrant images of inanimate objects, which in the hands of a skilful photographer often borders on fetishism. Food magazines, for example, will expend a great deal of time and attention on making the food look as desirable as possible – even to the extent of employing plenty of artificial ingredients and props.

## Shape and position

Just as variety in magazines comes from alternating photographs and other forms of illustration, so DTP software has made it easier than ever to experiment with the way that images are arranged on the page. It is much more common in magazines rather than newspapers to present photos in a dynamic fashion where images will be at angles or dominate much more of the page that would be given over to print in a paper.

Dramatic images can serve as the focal point for an introduction, taking up a page or the entirety of a double-page spread, with a standfirst appearing over the photograph. Alternatively, one useful approach is to use the image to break up the page, so that a small part is given over to white space and text while the rest is covered with a large, vivid photo.

**Figure 5.6** Experiment with position, shape and cropping of an image

Long, vertical pictures can have an unusual effect because we are so used to seeing images in landscape mode (which fits the way our peripheral vision works to 180 degrees in either direction). Including such an image in a feature immediately forces the reader's eyes to move up and down the page, enabling the designer to build and control such motion across a feature.

When including images, square images tend to be the dullest: rectangles are less symmetrical, and so attract attention to the page, and it is very common for tabloid-style magazines to employ a larger number of shapes (such as stars for celebrities) to create more visual impact. Even regular shapes, however, become much more interesting when laid out as a photomontage, for example, different locations in a city used as a mosaic in a travel feature. Such images become a sort of visual box or panel, with short captions providing important information to the reader in a fashion that can be taken in immediately.

In addition to considering where to place a photo, and what shape it should take, cropping an image can add greatly to its impact: the important detail needs to be framed in the picture. When taking photos, the photographer will spend a lot of time considering how the subject is framed, but it is not always possible, particularly on location, to get the perfect image. An editor or layout artist may take a photograph and simply use one part of it to create a stronger impression.

Zooming in on a subject is one way to add drama or excitement to an image, creating an unusual angle that can add suspense and tension. Too much, of course, and the image becomes unrecognisable, but it can also be necessary simply to remove redundant detail (such as additional figures who are not essential to the story).

## Special effects

Sometimes an image requires something different to make it stand out, such as filters that can be applied in an image editing program such as Photoshop. Prior to the widespread use of computers, filters had to be applied to camera lenses at the time of shooting (hence the name), or applied laboriously during the process of development.

This has changed dramatically in recent years, so the most unusual effects can be applied with a couple of mouse clicks. This said, the most outré filters tend not to appear in the vast majority of magazines, for the simple reason that they often look amateurish. Turning images into solarised, fish-eye lens monstrosities will not make a mediocre image look more interesting, but simply draw attention to the deficiencies of the original photograph.

Much more common is image tweaking, adjusting such things as the colour balance within an image or its contrast to bring out certain details. The attitude that the perfect photograph has to be captured on the spot is falling away: quite simply, Photoshop and other image editors provide useful tools that it is foolish for a photographer or designer to ignore, replacing the airbrush or developing room techniques that were often used to achieve similar effects but with much more effort.

However, it should always be recognised that no amount of tweaking can improve a bad image. Full-colour printing on glossy paper is a process that is very unforgiving and will reveal the faults in a poor photograph, so art editors will be looking for the best images that they can find.

## Film versus digital

Although there are many photographers working with film, with large-format cameras such as those which use 4 × 5 inch roll-film (and even larger, if rarer, models that can support prints of 8 × 10 inch film or more) being used to produce extremely high-quality photographs that can be blown up to cover a double-page spread.

However, the number of such photographers is decreasing. Digital SLR (single lens reflex) cameras were prohibitively expensive until very recently, and the quality of even the most expensive simply was not good enough for large images in glossy magazines. This has begun to change, however. Professional-level cameras capable of capturing 10-megapixel images (generally large enough even for an A4 print at high quality), are now available for less than £1,000, and at the time of writing 22-megapixel cameras have started to appear – although the price (£6,500 for a complete kit) means that these will be used by only a very few photographers.

Generally, though, film is slowly but steadily being replaced by digital cameras and quality is improving to such an extent that it is becoming very difficult to notice the difference between the two. While digital cameras can still be extremely expensive, the savings that are made in terms of production and convenience far outweigh this.

## Ethical considerations

The ability to adjust pictures to improve quality raises a number of questions about the ease with which digital manipulation of photographs can have ethical consequences.

Magazines, like newspapers, are often faced with the temptation to make the image say what they want it to say. In 2006, the CBS publicity magazine *Watch* included a photograph of one of its news anchors, Katie Couric, in which her neck and waistline had been raised to make her look thinner – a practice that is common for images included in fashion or men's magazines, but caused concern when applied to a picture for a serious publication.

But image manipulation predates digital technologies (which simply make the process easier). In 1989, *Time* magazine had a front cover image of Oprah Winfrey in which her head was spliced onto the body of another actress. The publication got into more trouble with its 1994 cover featuring O.J. Simpson, which was manipulated (digitally this time) to make the actor on trial for murder appear more menacing, according to critics.

The issue is less whether images are altered in themselves – this will happen to a lesser or greater degree with nearly all cover photographs, for example – than what the intended consequences are. Even without manipulation, an image may be used in such a way as to distort the truth, and this is the real ethical consideration.

When a photo is taken, the photographer selects what he or she considers most important about that scene. Likewise, when the image is cropped and framed in a magazine, that, in turn, may transform the reader's perception of an event. Images used for such things as publicity, celebrity or fashion are always going to be viewed differently to those that have a photojournalistic intention, which purport to document what has been going on at a specific time or place.

In addition, there are certain other considerations when using photos of individuals. Some of these, such as copyright, will be considered in Chapter 7, but it is worth bearing in mind some of the guidelines of the

PCC with regard to taking and using photographs. Thus it is unacceptable to photograph individuals in private places without their consent, and to continue photographing people when asked to stop can constitute harassment.

The most serious concerns, however, are around photographing children. Without even going into the murky waters of taste and decency (which have affected teen magazines at times in particular), no child under 16 should be photographed or interviewed without the consent of appropriate guardians or authorities (such as a school).

Finally, guidelines exist for obtaining photos by subterfuge, which will uphold a complaint against a title if it publishes photographs obtained by clandestine means.

## Picture editing

So far, this chapter has concentrated on the process of producing photographs for a magazine, but the role of picture editing is itself an important one. Some magazines will have a dedicated picture editor or researcher, while for others this will be as part of the remit of the art editor.

The first step in picture editing is very simple and concerns the quality of the image itself. As we have seen above, images are increasingly provided in digital format, but if they are slides they need to be viewed on a light box: any hint of poor quality, such as fuzziness or graininess, will be much worse when the image is blown up for print in a glossy magazine. For digital images, this involves the quality of the file, including its size and what compression if any has been used. Images that look fine on screen often appear terrible when printed (see Preparing images for print, p. 128).

As well as technical issues, there may be questions over the compositional competence of the image – for example, whether a lamp stand emerges from someone's head, or the quality of the lighting. Finally, when considering quality, there is also the issue of drama or impact: what does the image say to the reader that will improve the quality of the article? Sometimes, impact can override other technical considerations: a hasty, sub-paparazzi shot of a celebrity in a compromising position can be worth much more than a carefully framed studio shot, precisely because of its apparent amateurishness.

The fitness of a picture is an important part, then, of the overall effect of a magazine article. As it is often (alongside the title) the first thing noticed by the reader, the wrong picture can completely ruin an article by making it appear dull and uninteresting. Picture editing is thus a creative process, as well as often involving very routine administrative procedures such as organising couriers to bike pictures to and from a magazine and paying bills.

## Picture libraries

It is not always possible for a magazine to commission the right picture for the right time. If a title is running an article that has a historical focus, where the main actors are dead, for example, taking a photo of the person will be impossible. In addition, there are plenty of occasions when editors want to employ high-quality photography for an article that does not involve a specific individual or location, but where the designers wish to convey a certain theme visually.

It is for this reason that picture libraries and agencies such as Corbis have developed over the past few decades. These bring together huge collections of high-quality images – some of them iconic photographs of the nineteenth, twentieth and twenty-first centuries – and make them available (for a fee) to magazines and other publications. Increasingly these collections are available online, with editors able to browse through low-resolution thumbnails (these being unsuitable for print) to find the image they are looking for before paying for and downloading a high-quality version.

Press agencies are also another source of images. Part of their job will be to create and compile photographs of clients, although a downside of this is that the intention is to carefully control the public image of that client. If you are working for a celebrity magazine and want something different, the picture or art editor must be prepared to cultivate more 'obscure' sources who don't mind hanging around nightclubs until the small hours of the morning.

## Illustrations and graphics

While most of this chapter has concentrated on photography for magazines, alternative forms of illustration should never be forgotten.

As well as larger illustrations to accompany features, graphical elements are part of the branding that runs throughout a magazine.

As well as simply illustrating an article, graphic communication is intended to help a reader receive information as quickly as possible. Sometimes this works with very small elements that appear apparently incidentally on a page, such as a star-rating system with reviews that can convey at a glance what the reviewer thought of a topic. Elements such as icons or logos, may also help to orientate a reader in a magazine, guiding them through the navigation of different sections. Furthermore, graphics emphasise the corporate brand of the magazine, using logos and typography to emphasise that the title is a coherent entity.

When employing illustrators, some of this graphics work may be done in-house by the same artists who engage in layout, or freelances might be hired for a specific task. In contrast to photography, where there is usually some direct visual connection with the subject written about on the same pages, a drawing or piece of artwork offers the opportunity for a more abstract link to be made. This is not a strength of British consumer magazines today, although there are some better examples in the B2B sector where editors sometimes seek to spice up their copy with more interesting illustrations.

Although there are plenty of designers who will still draw their compositions by hand, the majority today will use computer applications such as Adobe Illustrator and Photoshop to produce their work. This has the added advantage of not requiring scanning at a later date and so can be delivered by disk or email to an art editor.

## Preparing images for print

When using images in a magazine, these must either be scanned in if provided in hard copy (such as artwork or image slides), or, if taken from a digital camera, converted to the appropriate format for print.

When scanning, images should never be scanned in the RGB (red, green, blue) format, but rather as CMYK (cyan, magenta, yellow, black) images so that they can be separated into different plates during printing. With hand-drawn artwork, the chances are that materials will be provided on paper or some similar medium that must be scanned in using a flatbed scanner. For photos, however, transparencies – either 35 mm slides or (better) 4 × 6 inch transparencies – should be used wherever possible to provide the best quality.

Scanners tend to use a number of set resolutions – the number of dots per inch (dpi) on screen or lines per inch on the printed page. Most monitors are set to a standard resolution of 72 dpi, but this should never be used when scanning for print: images scanned at this resolution will look fine on screen, but blurred or bitmapped when printed out. The minimum resolution for importing any image is 300 dpi.

Scanned images should then be saved as TIFF (tagged image file format) or EPS (encapsulated postscript) files, which will be recognised by more printing presses than any other format. Some printers will now accept JPEGs, but this is not advisable: JPEG files compress images by discarding information, which again can make an image that appears great on screen look blurry when printed on glossy paper.

Once images have been digitised, or imported from a digital camera, and are at the appropriate resolution, they must be converted from RGB to

**Figure 5.7** Photoshop enables users to separate out the colours of a digital image easily

CMYK if this has not already been done as part of the scanning process. In Photoshop, the industry standard for preparing images, this is done by going to Image, Mode, CMYK on the menu.

However, there are also more advanced options for designers with a properly calibrated monitor (that is, one set to display proper contrast, brightness and colour management). Paper types – whether coated or uncoated – and different colour stocks (some have a more yellowish tinge) can affect the final output of a magazine, and later versions of Photoshop include an option for 'soft-proofing'. This is accessed by going to View, Proof Setup on the menu and selecting CMYK from the custom proof drop-down list. This will then offer a series of 'proof conditions', such as paper stock and the option to simulate the paper colour.

## The cover

As already discussed in Chapter 3, the cover is the most important element for selling a magazine on the newsstand. While the building blocks that go into a successful cover for different magazines operating in diverse markets would take too much space to cover in detail here, there are common features that do work across nearly all of them.

**An eye-catching photograph or illustration:** rather than a montage, this nearly always consists of an A4 size image that covers most, if not all, of the front cover, and is appropriate for the audience under consideration. As noted before, consumer magazines in particular tend to be very similar (and thus rather conservative) in their choice of cover models so that – by image alone – it can be very difficult to distinguish one title from another.

Research by Comag in the 1990s, which, as Morrish (2003) points out, was rather limited, suggested that men expect a cover to have something to do with the contents, but women do not. More importantly, a competent cover picture will be clear but not crowded, and ideally work with three bright colours to attract the reader's attention.

**Cover lines:** these are extremely important in making readers pick up a title, and so need to be short (so that they do not crowd out the main image) but punchy, conveying the meaning of an article concisely. Some titles may include page numbers, but better practice is to offer an innovative cover title that leads the reader onto the contents page where they will look up the story while browsing. Once they have it in their hands, they are more likely to purchase the magazine.

There has been some debate about the significance of differences between cover lines and actual story titles. It is not uncommon for the two not to match up precisely – the words that appear on a cover may be fewer

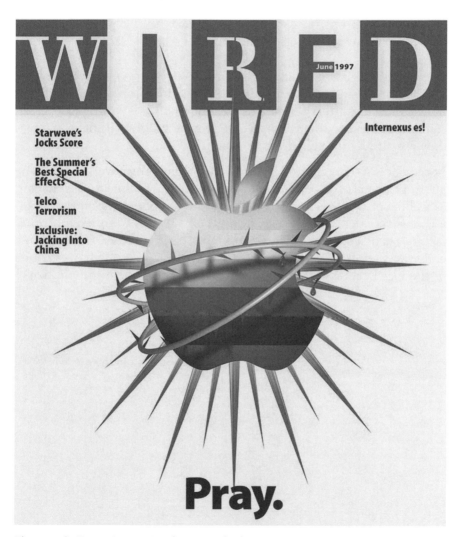

**Figure 5.8** Sometimes simplicity works best on a cover

words in larger print to grab the reader's attention. Too much variance, however, and this can be frustrating in that the reader may not know where the article appears inside the magazine.

**Title:** the title of a magazine serves an important function as a logo, branding the magazine. Its position, nearly always in the top quarter of a front cover, also serves a practical purpose. When publications are stacked one on top of the other in a newsagent or supermarket, this will be the only part of the magazine that can be seen clearly by a prospective buyer. As such, bright bold colours and clear typography that can be read from a distance are essential.

A cover, then, is a combination of image and type – an image on its own, however striking, is unlikely to say anything to the reader. Cover lines provide a context for the picture, one that should intrigue a person standing at the newsstand and, ideally, provide an unusual angle on topics they are already interested in.

Because it is so important in selling the magazine, the cover – combining all the elements of colour, image and typography discussed in this chapter, as well as principles of design that are the subject of the next chapter – is usually designed (or at least overseen) by the art editor. While other factors such as seasonal variations and poor weather or economic conditions affect sales to a lesser or greater degree, a poor cover is one of the biggest mistakes that an editorial and art department can make.

# 6

# Layout, print and post-production

So far we have looked at written and graphical content separately. Now it is time to bring them together in the final layout of a magazine, and follow through the magazine production process to the final printing and binding of a title.

## The role of the production editor

The production editor is the final key role in terms of magazine production. On smaller magazines, the position may be taken by the editor, but for larger titles there will be a separate production editor whose task is to ensure that all deadlines are met and that all stages of the workflow progress as smoothly as possible.

While the strategy of editorial planning is the responsibility of the editor (which is why it was introduced in Chapter 4), day-to-day maintenance of the flat-plan will fall under the remit of the production editor. He or she provides a strong link between the editorial and art departments, ensuring that copy is passed on for layout and then on to sub-editors (for whom he or she will have managerial responsibility).

As well as working with the sections of a magazine responsible for words and visuals, the production editor will have to liaise with the advertising department. As pointed out in Chapter 4, the flat-plan does not simply include editorial pages but also the position of ads, and films or files for these will need to come in at set deadlines to be passed on to the printer.

This leads to the final major responsibility of the production editor: to engage with the printer. The production editor will need to collect mechanical data from the printer (page sizes and file types, for example) and ensure that the relevant material is ready to go to press, whether film or digital files.

## DTP

DTP, or desktop publishing, is essential to modern magazine design. While occasionally a title will use traditional composition methods, these really have no place any more in the professional publishing world and DTP is a fundamental skill for many people working with magazines. When titles need to employ a layout artist, they will hire designers as the best suited to the job, but it is increasingly important for even editors and other journalists to know their way around a DTP package: for those starting out in a publishing career, it can be very useful when landing a subbing job or making amendments to a feature.

DTP, the skills involved in laying out designs using a computer, can encompass more than paper-based publications such as magazines, newspapers or books, to incorporate web sites, retail packaging and promotional items. It began in 1985 when Aldus (later to merge with Adobe) released PageMaker for the Apple Mac, the first software program to allow WYSIWYG (what you see is what you get) layout on screen.

Early software was very primitive by today's standards, but new technology was increasingly being used in newsrooms by the end of the 1980s and saw a real boom in the 1990s as computer prices dropped and more and more companies saw the virtue of streamlining design.

Although often associated with graphic design, the latter refers more to the creative process of coming up with ideas for presentation, whereas DTP is more concerned with the mechanical process of laying out those ideas. For magazines, it brings together the elements of text, image and colour considered in the previous chapter.

## QuarkXPress versus Adobe InDesign

Although not the first DTP package to be released, for more than a decade magazine design has been dominated by QuarkXPress. The program was launched in 1987 for the Apple Macintosh, followed by a version

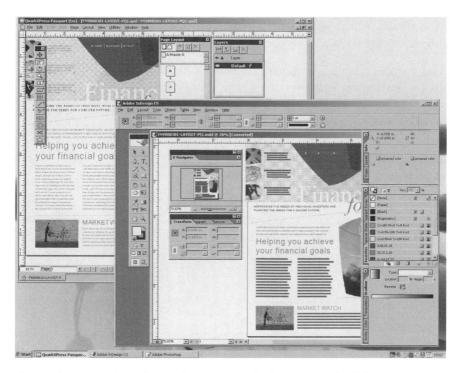

**Figure 6.1** Examples of page layouts in QuarkXPress and Adobe InDesign

for Windows in 1992 that was largely neglected until the early 2000s. By 1996, with version 3.3, Quark was seen as a stable and reliable program and by that time had become an industry standard.

Part of the early success of Quark lay in the fact that it could be modified to include additional features via a system known as XTensions, but more than anything else it combined a simple interface with reliability. However, the fact that it had gained a 90 per cent market share by the end of the 1990s, its very high price and slow development times led to charges that it had become a monopoly. In 1999, Adobe released InDesign as a direct competitor to Quark.

Although substantially cheaper, InDesign initially did not particularly appeal to designers. This changed with the release of InDesign 2.0, launched at the same time as QuarkXPress 5.5 in 2002: while Adobe's program supported Apple's new MacOS X, Quark did not. More significantly, InDesign included support for PDF (Portable Document Format) as standard, which had begun to transform the way that magazines and other documents were prepared for press.

The current version of Quark (7.3 at the time of writing) can now import and export PDF files directly, and has received much more favourable reviews in recent years. Many also prefer its way of distinguishing between content (such as text or image boxes) and objects, which is the mode used to position those boxes and other items on the page. Certainly for those who have worked with Quark for a long time, its interface appears much more intuitive.

However, InDesign (currently version CS3) supported advanced features such as better transparency options at an earlier stage, and was also compatible with the other designer favourite, Photoshop. A more competitive price and better support for PDF means that InDesign has finally started to overtake Quark as the industry favourite for magazine design.

## Visualisation

While most design will take place in a DTP package such as Quark or InDesign, making a mock-up of a page is a useful exercise. The task for a designer, as Frost (2003) points out, is to produce a page that is both original and stays in the house style. With a little experience, creating a visual on a scrap of paper enables the designer to work out the plan for a page in a matter of minutes.

Taking a piece of paper, the visual can be used to give a rough idea of how the main elements of the page will fit together. Once a basic plan is in place, frames and boxes can be laid out in a DTP program.

The visual is usually done on a piece of A4 so that it is roughly the size of the final page as it will appear in the magazine. To this can be added the title, standfirst, and then columns and boxes outlined for text and pictures, so that the designer can experiment with such things as the placement and size of photos, or have a rough idea of whether two or three columns of text will look better on the page.

In many cases, a visual may be more than enough to get the ideas required to start laying out the next page. The next step, however, can be to move onto a draft, an accurate representation on the page that will show more precisely where each element has to go.

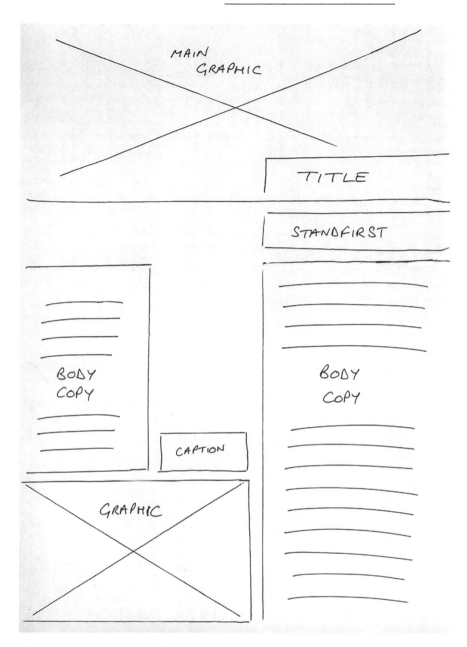

**Figure 6.2** An example of a visual

## Using the grid

Central to most modern magazine design is the grid – which has become almost synonymous with the professional approach. The purpose of the grid is to provide a basic template that will enable consistency across the magazine. If every page starts from scratch, although individually this could result in fabulous and exciting designs, the overall effect for the magazine would be to make it look much more amateurish.

The grid becomes the outline on which can be laid all other elements of the page – the title, columns and images, as well as any boxouts or other components. Certain features, such as page numbers or a magazine logo, will always appear in the same place so that the reader can navigate through pages easily, but others, such as images, will be laid out in different positions so that there is also some variety. The point of the grid is to provide a bedrock for the rest of magazine design, not to enforce dull and sterile conformity across every page.

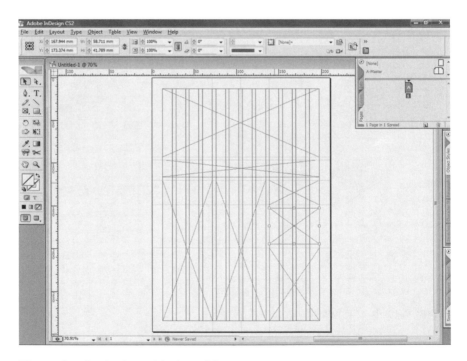

**Figure 6.3** Designing with the grid

Ideally, the grid should correspond to some kind of ratio, dividing the page in halves, thirds or quarters. It will establish column positions and also gutters between those columns and a margin around the edge of the page. A slightly more complex but commonly employed grid is to divide the page by the ratio of $1:1.414$, which corresponds to the ratio of the width of an A4 page to its length. This divides the page into four equal quarters, which can then be further divided into equal sections using the same ratio.

As the basis for creative and professional design, the grid will provide a series of lines on the page that can be used effectively for variety within proportion. For example, a very commonly employed grid divides the page into 12 columns: no magazine will ever print 12 columns of text – you would be lucky to get more than a couple of words to each line. However, what this basic grid does is enable the designer to set one page out with two columns, another with three and yet another with four – an easy way to distinguish a lead-in page from other articles, or from news stories. While the column widths will vary from story to story, they will still remain in proportion to each other as long as they follow the grid.

Once a grid is in place, items should be aligned to the guide lines consistently: if items hang over grid lines or move from place to place for no reason, this will fail to create a harmonious impression across a magazine. Actually, good designers will sometimes 'jump the grid', staggering a page element across the page in an unexpected manner – but they know why they want to do this because they are used to creating pages that create variety within a consistent framework.

## Master pages and templates

DTP packages allow designers to create master pages. These are not printed out, but once a grid and overall style is determined, these contain information that will be used in the rest of the magazine. There will be a master page for the left-hand and right-hand pages of the publication, each of which contains placeholders for such things as page numbers, logos and other material that typically goes into the header and footer of a page.

Templates are the next step up from a master page, and a title will probably use several of these for different types of article or different sections of a magazine. Rather than designing each page from scratch,

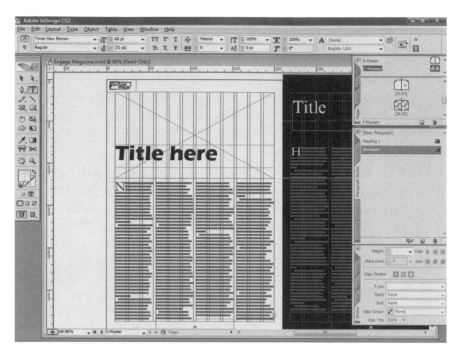

**Figure 6.4** A master page in InDesign

the layout artist will open a template and begin to drop copy and photos onto the screen – this allows him or her to experiment with the presentation while maintaining overall consistency with other pages.

The template will contain the grid with specified columns, and may have sample holders for text, headings and illustrations. For example, it might be the house style always to begin with an image in the top right- or left-hand corner of a page, and headings will probably appear in the same spot so that they do not jump up and down from feature to feature.

The problem with this approach is that while it makes a publication look much smoother and professional, it can also result in pages looking very similar and thus a little dull. The task for a good designer is to make proper use of a template to prevent a magazine looking as though it was thrown together in a chaotic fashion, but templates should also serve as a launch pad for experimenting with different areas of design.

## Style sheets

Along with templates, style sheets are another tool within DTP packages that can help to speed up design. Style sheets are used to provide default settings for text in headers, standfirsts, body copy, paragraphs and so on.

For example, you may decide that the standard font for body copy in features is 9 point Garamond on a 9.5 point body and with a 3 point space at the beginning of paragraphs. Likewise, subheadings may be 10 point Helvetica on an 11 point body in a different hue to the rest of the text. These elements can be entered into the style palette in Quark or InDesign and saved: when a designer wishes to create a subheading or paragraph of body text, he or she simply selects one of those entries so that formatting is applied automatically and quickly.

As with templates, style sheets will be set up early in the life of a magazine and not tinkered with too much unless the publication undergoes a substantial redesign.

## Headings and intros

The previous chapter discussed the use of typography as a visual element on a page, but it is also important to discuss how titles and standfirsts work as building blocks in the design of the page.

The headline is, alongside any large images, the most important element for attracting the reader's attention. It has to convey information about the article in a very limited number of words and, unsurprisingly, must be considerably larger than the surrounding text to draw in the reader's eye as he or she is leafing through a publication.

Verbally, of course, titles must be appropriate to the audience of the magazine: serious and sober publications may appreciate some subtle wordplay, but while 'Meet the shadow minister for militant Islam' immediately has a great deal to say for the readers of *The Spectator*, it is much less effective for the audience of *Nuts* than 'Sexy celebs caught topless', which graced the cover feature of the issue that appeared at the same time.

Typically, the headline will appear at the top of the page – although if there is a strong graphic image it may appear immediately beneath this. Sometimes, for variety, a magazine will try running the headline through or alongside body copy – but this is nearly always confusing for the reader. What can be more successful, however, is to place the main headline beneath a standfirst: while this is not as logical to read as following on with the intro, it can make for a bold design if used relatively sparingly.

In magazines (in contrast to some parts of newspapers), headlines outside the news pages at least tend to run across columns and only be one or two lines deep. Usually the headline is in a different colour from the main body copy – indeed, should be in a different colour to make it stand out as the reader glances from page to page. While there is no hard and fast rule as to whether a headline should be sans serif or not, it is certainly the case that it will often be bolder to help emphasise the words.

The shape of the headline, as well as the standfirst or intro, is important, in giving balance to a page. Standfirsts are usually presented as blocks of text that work as a graphical object in their own right, adding a dash of colour and visual interest to a page. As well as standing out visually, they also present concise information that will expand on the title and present the reader with key features that will help him or her decide whether to continue reading.

## Mechanical specifications: margins, bleed and trim size

When laying out pages, the columns and graphics that go into most articles will need to have a margin around the page. Unlike newspapers, however, where this margin is designed to allow some leeway when printing at high speeds, margins are added to magazine pages for aesthetic effect. White space around the edge of text and between columns makes text easier to read.

For some pages, however, particularly those with a background colour or illustrations that run over the entire spread or just part of it, ink will need to go right up to the edge of the page for the best effect. This is referred to as 'bleed', and means that in a design program such as Quark or InDesign, colour is taken over the actual edge of the page, typically to a distance of 5 mm or so beyond the trim marks.

Printers are able to cope with this because printing takes place on pieces of paper that are larger than the final page size of the magazine (usually 20 mm larger on each side). Trim size refers to the actual dimensions of this final page, which gives the canvas for designers and layout artists

**Figure 6.5** Bleed and trim marks on a layout (left); the trimmed page (right)

to work with. Crop marks, or small crossed lines, are placed at the corners of the page to indicate where the page should be trimmed.

Finally, the other mechanical specification that can affect the way pages are laid out is gutter width. This is the fold where pages meet, and varies according to the type of binding that is used to hold the magazine together, whether it is perfect binding (glue) or saddle stitched with staples. In different parts of a magazine, particularly larger publications that are perfect bound, some pages will look further apart and so the gutter width will need to be changed to take this into account. Unless you are creating a double-page spread with an image that runs across both pages, no content should go into the gutter as it will generally be unreadable.

## Prepress

Although, strictly speaking, prepress refers to the entire design process from laying out pages to sending them to the press, here we shall restrict the term to the stage of magazine preparation that takes place after page design and before files are sent to a printer. Today, this can be simplified to a degree to mean checking through PDF documents so that they have the best chance of being printed correctly.

Prior to the widespread use of DTP, prepress involved a wide range of mechanical and technical skills, such as typesetting and paste-up, where text and images would be laid by hand onto a board to create camera-ready copy – a single page that could be photographed and films sent to the printer.

Digital prepress involves fewer people and is much quicker (at least for a skilled layout artist). There is no literal cutting and pasting onto board, and file preparation involves either getting ready a file that can be sent directly to the printers or printing out a camera-ready page that can be photographed.

The stage of getting files ready to send to a printer is also sometimes referred to as 'preflight', and is often carried in specialist software. When laying out a page, various fonts and images need to be collected together and other checks made to prepare the layout for print. These include:

- Checking that true bold or italic fonts are used. DTP programs, like word processors, can apply bold or italic styles to just about any font. However, only some fonts have a separate set of characters in italic or bold (true as opposed to false styles). On a desktop printer controlled by the PC, this is rarely a problem, but when files are sent to a commercial printer the fonts may not print correctly.
- Including the right fonts with a file. The use of PDF has greatly improved this process, but it can still be a problem when files are sent to a printer without the correct fonts, for which another font will be substituted, potentially ruining the design. In some cases with Type 1 fonts, this means sending both the version that appears on the screen and the print version. Fonts can be collected together in software, or must be copied manually from the fonts folder onto the disk that includes the page layout file.
- Ensuring that crop marks and bleed allowances are in the correct position so that when the page is trimmed colour will run to the edge of the page.
- Ensuring that all graphics are included. When a DTP package works with images on screen, it shows a low-resolution version on screen that looks fine but will be very poor quality when printed. All original images must be included with the final file and in the correct format for print (TIFF or EPS file formats, CMYK, not RGB).

- Checking for potential RIP errors. If the file has to be ripped to film, that is, converted into a bitmap image to be output onto a photographic negative, errors can occur when files become too large, there are complex blends of colours on the page, or Postscript Type 1 and TrueType fonts are used on the same page.
- Extraneous elements on the page – those that typically have been moved to the pasteboard (the non-printable part of the screen in a DTP program) – need to be removed before the file is sent to print. Leaving them in increases file sizes and can cause problems with printing.
- Complex effects, such as transparency (where part of an underlying image should show through) need to be checked. Often these rely on building up layers in an image, but the image should be 'flattened' in a program such as Photoshop or Illustrator, that is, made into one single layer, so that potential problems are minimised.
- Trapping settings must be verified, to ensure that there will be no ugly white spaces or badly overlapping colours on the page.
- It is good practice to set up a system of file names that is agreed with the printer. For example, a system that goes along the lines of publisher_titlename_issuenumber.pdf will help to indicate to the printer that he has received the correct file.

The PPA includes a useful checklist that has been standardised with many UK printers and publishers, called Pass4Press, at www.pass4press.com/public/downloads/pass4press_v7_apps.pdf.

## Digital versus film

Until very recently, every magazine would need to send a copy of any DTP files to a repro house, where these files would be fed through a machine to output a negative image of the file on film, a process known as ripping to film, from RIP, raster image processing. This involves taking a vector image (such as the mathematical information that describes a font) and converting it into a raster or bitmap, a series of dots that can be output onto the film negative.

This negative is then sent to the printer and, through the photo-lithographic process, transferred onto plate as a positive. As part of offset printing, the inked positive image is then transferred to a rubber roll as a negative, and finally back onto the page the right way round.

Today, this process has been supplemented – or even replaced – by other methods that reduce the need to create a photographic negative. Computer to Plate (CTP, sometimes referred to as direct to plate printing) allows a digital file to be delivered directly to the plate, removing the requirement for a negative. A related process is Direct Digital Printing (DDP), which again does not require film and is often achieved with high-quality, commercial laser printers that do not even require plates to be made.

The past few years have seen something of a mini-revolution in the printing process, with digital technologies replacing film for many publishers. The advantages of moving to digital are as follows:

- Cost savings (after the initial investment on the part of the printer). Film does not need to be duplicated, and it is much cheaper to transfer files either across the Internet or on storage media such as DVD.
- Shorter production cycles. As film does not need to be sent through the post, or files sent to a repro house and then returned to the publisher for checking, time can be shaved off the production cycle. If these time savings are used to reduce the time between accepting material and sending it off to print, however, then the production editor will need to keep a closer eye on deadlines.
- The move to soft proofing, again with time and cost savings, as well as the possibility for remote proofing, where changes made to the printer's copy can be viewed electronically.

## Digitial distribution methods: TIFF/IT and PDF

When sending files digitally, there are two main choices: TIFF/IT and PDF. TIFF/IT is an international standard for prepress exchange that bundles together a page as a tagged image file format, but which also includes additional information on such things as colour encoding and separation. It is typically not used for the final stages of the production cycle, but usually midway through the process, when an advertiser has to send a layout for inclusion in a magazine, for example.

While TIFF/IT has been accepted as a standard across the print industry, the fact that it produces large file sizes and is hard to edit once compressed, makes it much less widely used than Adobe's portable document format

(PDF). PDF is widely supported across a variety of computer platforms, such as Mac and PC, it offers much better compression for sending online, can include both low- and high-resolution images in the same file (for proofing on screen and for print), and allows some limited editing to take place after the file has been saved in PDF format.

PDF was introduced by Adobe in 1993, but did not really transform the business of printing until the end of the 1990s. It consists of a complete description of a document that is device independent: in other words, it does not matter which computer it is written on or which printer it is output to. As long as software is in place that can read the PDF file, it will produce an accurate rendition of the page.

The PDF format includes some of Adobe's PostScript language, which has long been the standard for describing how pages are output to digital printers. (PostScript itself is gradually being replaced by PDF.) In addition, PDF files include a means to embed fonts into a document, so that these can be sent more easily to print.

Things that can go wrong with a PDF include images being too low resolution for print, fonts not being embedded (so that another font is substituted on the printer's machine), wrong colours being assigned and too much compression resulting in 'artefacts' appearing (blurred pixels that reduce the quality of the image). This is why prepress preparation is extremely important.

Sometimes you may see reference to component files or elements: these are the various images and page files that may exist in a variety of formats (such as TIFFs and JPEGs for images, or Quark and Adobe files). This is not the ideal way to produce a file that can be sent to the printer for easy digital printing, and so they should be converted as part of the prepress process into PDF or TIFF/IT.

## Proofing

Proofing is often closely tied to the subbing process outlined in Chapter 4, whereby an editor will proof-read articles to check for accuracy and consistency. Indeed, the terms are often used synonymously, but here the term proofing (as opposed to proofreading) means checking the final layout of pages for such things as colour accuracy.

Text proofreading can take place with an in-house laser printer. To cut costs (and waste) more subbing may take place on screen these days, but at some point editors and subs will probably wish to print off a hard copy to double check, particularly as it is easier to read substantial quantities of text on paper rather than on screen.

A printer will want some type of guarantee from the publisher that the files delivered to them for printing will be as accurate as possible. Any changes made after delivery will incur extra costs, and the printer also wishes to determine that any mistakes on the final page are (barring failures in the mechanical process such as misaligned plates) the responsibility of the publisher.

This is why proofing the final artwork is so important. The preflight checks listed previously are intended to identify any potential problems such as mismatched colours or transparency effects that do not work, blocking out text or graphics on the page.

It is worth bearing in mind the limitations of proofs: because of possible small variations in inks and papers used during the printing process, pages cannot always look exactly the same. These variations can exist even between the same types of press (though to a much lesser degree), but most proofs will be produced on a different system. Nonetheless, proofing is still extremely important to minimise unpleasant surprises before printing begins.

## Types of proofs

Of the types of proofing available to publishers, press proofing will almost certainly be the most accurate because it is taken from a press that uses the same plates and inks as will be used in the final version. More economical means of proofing will not use the same press, but provide 'contract' proofs that provide halftone dot patterns very similar to those used in the final version.

Sometimes proofs will be produced as high-quality, laminated sheets of paper, with brand names such as Cromalin and Matchprint. These use the same colour separation film negatives as are used in the final printing process, and so can give a very accurate impression of how the page should appear.

In recent years, however, there has been a move towards so called 'soft proofing', that is, using the monitor to make final decisions about colour and density on screen. Such soft proofing can never completely match the printed page, because of the way the human eye sees colour reflected off paper as opposed to shining from a screen, but there have been developments that do make it possible to reflect how a page will appear more accurately than before.

For soft proofing to be at all accurate, the monitor must be calibrated as described in Chapter 5. While the process can never be perfect, it is becoming more and more acceptable to many graphics professionals as reliability increases, and is also helpful in making the proofing process much faster, without the need to courier pages back and forth between printer and publisher.

## Printing

Once a magazine has been proofed and all preflight checks carried out, it is ready to be sent to the printer: for the production department, the issue is 'closed'. For traditional methods, this involves bundling up editorial and advertising films and sending them through the post. Digital files must be sent online or on some form of storage media, usually CD or DVD. Once a file is accepted for printing, it is deemed as 'gone to bed' and can no longer be modified.

For platemaking involving film, the film is placed in a vacuum frame to hold it against a photosensitive blank plate. A powerful light is shone onto the film and plate, so that it holds an image from the film that can then be cleaned and dried ready for printing. As four, eight or 16 pages will be printed at once, so multiple films are 'stripped-up', placed together so that they can be made into a single plate that will run through the press.

Printing methods that make use of computer to plate (CTP) do away with the need to transfer an image from the film to the plate. A laser burns a copy of the file onto the plate, removing the need for negative or positive films (depending on the process being used in more traditional methods).

When CTP began to be used in the early 1990s, plates would be coated with silver-halide that was sensitive to the visible light from a laser.

The next step was to use what are called 'thermal ablative' plates: these are aluminium plates with two layers – an 'oleophilic' layer, that is one that attracts oil, and a 'hydrophilic' layer, attracting water, beneath it. The laser used in this process generates heat to burn off parts of the top layer (the 'ablative') to create an image from the digital file. This technique has the advantage that after the image is created, the plate requires no further processing with chemicals but is merely washed to remove any excess ablative material.

More recently, manufacturers have started to work with plastic plates. These are less durable than metal ones, but can work well (and much more cheaply) for small print runs.

Once plates have been made, the most typical method for actual printing is what is called offset (or offset litho) printing. As part of this process, drawing on the fact that water and oil do not mix, wet plates are inked with the oily ink sticking only to the raised part of the plate and being rejected by the non-image area that retains a coating of water.

The plate, on a rolling cylinder, runs through rollers connected to a water tray first and then through rollers connected to an ink tray. From here, the image is transferred to a rubber blanket and then to paper. This is done four times, for each of the four colours used in full-colour printing. As the paper is wet from so much water and ink, there is a danger of smudging and so the paper then passes through an oven before finally being run through refrigerated metal chill rollers that cool the paper and make the ink set.

For large-scale printing, the process used to print thousands of pages per hour is called web offset litho printing. This is because paper is transferred to the printing press from a huge roll (or web) of paper, weighing anything up to a ton. As each roll of paper can be spliced together with another, the printing press does not need to stop working once plates are in place and a job is started.

The alternative form of press is a sheet-fed press which, as the name suggests, prints on individual sheets of paper and will usually be a smaller press, printing fewer pages per hour.

The budget set by the publisher will determine how many copies are produced by the printer, but in some cases there will also be an 'overrun', additional extra copies that are charged to the publisher at a different rate.

## Binding and finishing

After a magazine has been printed, the final stage is to bind and finish the copies for distribution.

Magazine finishing refers to the process of folding, trimming and binding the magazine, rather than embossing or adding special finishes to the paper as it does in other types of printing. Finishing will be done either in-line, as part of the mechanical process of printing (usually the case with web presses) or off-line, when the paper is taken away and the final stages of production carried out on other machines.

Folding is often done in-line, with the multiple pages on a single sheet being folded into a signature. These signatures are then gathered together in receptacles called pockets or hoppers for binding, being either staple bound (also called saddle-stitch binding, because the pages fan out like a saddle and would previously have been sewn together) or perfect bound. The latter is better for magazines larger than 50 pages or so, and involves the spine edge of the signatures being ground perfectly flat before glue is applied to hold them together in the cover. Publishers tend to prefer perfect binding (if their publication is large enough to support it) because additional information can be printed on the spine.

If the cover is printed on the same type of paper as that used in the magazine's interior, this is known as a self-cover. After this, the magazine is trimmed: at this stage, the pages of the signature are still attached to each other, so these have to be slit open and the magazine cut down to its appropriate dimensions along the height and width.

Today, all of this process is mechanised – whether in-line or off-line – and the savings and efficiency of this mechanisation is one reason why magazines can customise content. Sometimes this takes place with different versions of a magazine, for regional markets, for example (more common in the US, with its much larger market in terms of both geography and population, than the UK), or to create different issues for subscribers and newsstand readers.

Another step for some magazines is special pages, for example with scratch and sniff cards, or cover mounts. Where possible, these will be done as part of the in-line printing and binding process, but others – such as attaching cover-mounted CDs – must be done separately, either by an automated process or by hand.

After all these stages, the magazine is finally ready for distribution to wholesalers, and then on to individual readers via newsstand sales or posting through the mail to subscribers.

# 7
# Legal and ethical issues

Many of the regulatory issues that affect magazines are similar to those across the media industry. This chapter offers a summary of the legal restraints that all editors and publishers have to consider with regard to defamation, copyright, data protection, fair comment and privacy. For a more detailed consideration of legal issues, the reader should also consult *McNae's Essential Law for Journalists* (Welsh *et al.* 2007) and *Magazine Law* (Mason and Smith 1998).

Some areas of legislation, such as DA (Defence Advisory) Notices, the Human Rights Act and court reporting, are generally more important to newspapers than magazines (other than specialist interest titles), and so are not dealt with in any great detail here. As well as the law, however, journalists also need to consider ethical and professional codes of conduct for the material that they publish.

## Defamation

Laws against defamation, principally the UK Defamation Act 1996, are intended to protect the reputation of an individual against unjustified and unwarranted attacks. Any communication that is held to damage a reputation is considered defamatory even if it is fiction, meaning that such things as television plays and magazine short stories fall under the remit of the law if they are seen to harm an individual.

While there have been various criticisms of the harshness of the UK defamatory laws, in principle their purpose is to balance the right of a person to protect his or her reputation against the defence of freedom of speech and expression. As Mason and Smith observe (1998: 8):

> The real skill in journalism does not show simply in the cleverness of the ways of defending an action for defamation once it has been published, but in recognising a possible problem *before publication*, and then in handling it in such a way that any complaint after publication can be successfully rebutted or defended.

The maxim should be: 'If in doubt find out' rather than 'If in doubt leave it out'.

Defamation is held to have taken place if a person is exposed to hatred, contempt or ridicule, is shunned or avoided after publication, discredited in a business or profession, and generally lowered in the eyes of the public in an unwarranted fashion.

Unlike other criminal and civil actions, where burden of proof rests on the prosecution or plaintiff, in UK libel laws the burden of proof rests on the defendant. The plaintiff does have to prove, however, that any defamatory statements will be reasonably understood to refer to him or her, and that they are communicated to a third person (which is not difficult in the case of libel as words are recorded in print or other permanent form).

The 1996 law did clear up one important area regarding who could be sued: in the past, this could be anyone involved in distribution of material, such as printers and newsagents, but since 1996 this has been restricted to the authors, editors or publishers of defamatory material.

What is more, the author of a defamatory statement is the person who originated that statement, but may defend him or herself if that statement was never intended for publication, for example in a private diary.

## Libel and slander

There are two types of defamation: slander, which is a communication by word of mouth, and libel, which relates to publication in print or a more permanent form such as a broadcast.

Libel is more serious for a magazine because obviously that deals with publication. In addition, slander needs to be made in the presence of witnesses for a prosecution to succeed. A journalist may still slander an individual, however, for example, simply by talking about someone in the presence of others in a defamatory manner or via telephone calls to a third party.

In libel cases the plaintiff does not need to prove that he or she suffered monetary losses as a result of the publication, although slander does require this proof unless they have been accused of a criminal action, having a contagious disease, being accused of unchastity or adultery in the case of a woman, or attacked on the basis of their profession. In both libel and slander, the plaintiff may bring a case even if they have not been named. If it is held that a reasonable individual could infer the identity of the person from an article or statement, then the law is likely to uphold their complaint.

## Truth and privilege

The ultimate defence against libel is truth, referred to legally as justification: a statement may be damaging to an individual's reputation, but if it is true then it is not defamatory. However, if the statement refers to a conviction regarded as 'spent' under the Rehabilitation of Offenders Act 1974, or is a criminal libel, it may be considered libellous if prompted through malice.

Criminal libel is rarely invoked in the UK, unless the libel is held to be so serious that criminal proceedings will best serve the public interest. Mason and Smith give the example of allegations in *Private Eye* in 1975 that were seen to link Sir James Goldsmith to Lord Lucan, then the subject of a murder investigation. The case was dropped when *Private Eye* withdrew the statements and publicly apologised.

Libel proceedings cannot be brought against the dead in civil law (which covers most cases in the UK), although it is possible under criminal libel if statements are shown to affect living relatives or potentially cause a breach of the peace.

Journalists may publish defamatory material safely under the defence of absolute or qualified privilege. The first relates to reporting court cases that deal with alleged crimes, where journalits must be protected from the threat of defamation in order to report what they see as the truth. However, if a journalist reports evidence ruled as inadmissible, he or she may be guilty of contempt of court, and so in danger of prosecution.

Qualified privilege covers reports of public proceedings, such as public inquiries and conferences, as well as court cases, as well as documents required to be open to public inspection such as statements produced by members of government. However, the defence of qualified privilege might be lost if reporting is shown to be motivated by malice or is inaccurate. Likewise, if the plaintiff asked for a contradictory statement to be published (denying any defamatory comments) and this is not included in publication, qualified privilege may also be revoked.

## Malicious falsehoods and fair comment

While issues of absolute and qualified privilege tend to affect newspaper journalists more than those working for magazines, this is not the case for reviewers, who may often be affected by cases brought against them.

When testing or reviewing products, journalists, editors and publishers may face a prosecution for malicious falsehood, sometimes called 'trade libels'. If a review disparages the goods that a person produces or trades in a defamatory manner, it is not a libel but a malicious falsehood. If, however, the review goes on to suggest incorrectly that the fault of the goods is due to the professional character of that person, then it becomes a libel.

In a case of malicious falsehood, the burden of proof that a statement is untrue falls on the plaintiff, who must also demonstrate damages such as financial loss. In addition, malice must be proved in this type of case, and while a libel suit ends with the death of either the plaintiff or defendant, cases of malicious falsehood can be carried on by representatives of the deceased.

Defence against malicious falsehood requires the defendant to prove the accuracy of any tests he or she may have carried out, following any instructions regarding testing to the letter. When making adverse claims against competing products, the reviewer should be certain that he or she is really comparing like with like.

While malicious falsehood tends to refer to product testing, libel is more likely to be invoked for other types of reviews where an individual is involved, for example, music or film reviewing.

In such cases, a reviewer may be able to invoke the defence of fair comment: this means that the reviewer offered his or her honest opinion of events, persons or products (including the fact that he or she did not like them, or believe them of suitable quality – the most important task of the reviewer as we saw in Chapter 4). However, this cannot be used as a defence if the journalist gets facts wrong or if comments can be shown to be irresponsible or motivated by malice.

## Professional indemnity

This chapter has considered libel and malicious falsehood in some detail because the consequences of getting it wrong can be very serious for a publication. Payments can be severely damaging to the reputation of a title as well as its finances. Roman Polanski won £50,000 in a libel suit from *Vanity Fair* for an article in 2002 that made him appear 'callously indifferent', in his words, to the death of his former wife, Sharon Tate. More recently *OK!* magazine was forced to pay undisclosed damages to the actor David Hasselhof after claiming he was drunk and abusive in a nightclub.

Sometimes libel payments can run to extremes. An Indonesian court ordered *Time* magazine to pay more than $100 million in damages for an article about former President Suharto, although *Time* was still contesting that action. It is more common for libel payments to be revised downwards, for example from £600,000 to £60,000 paid by *Private Eye* to Sonia Sutcliffe, wife of the Yorkshire Ripper.

Yet damages are only part of the problem for titles faced with a libel suit. In another case, again with *Private Eye* (one of the most sued magazines in the world), a suit brought by a Cornish accountant against the magazine was thrown out of court because the plaintiff, Stuart Condliffe, declared himself bankrupt and was thus unable to pay legal fees.

Because of this, there are several legal companies that offer Professional Indemnity and Public Liability Insurance. In most cases, this will offer to cover potential costs in the case of libel, but also protection for infringement of copyright and breach of confidentiality.

While this offers a degree of reassurance to a number of publishers and editors (and increasingly writers who find that they may be sued), some working in the industry consider insurance to be a double-edged sword. Because of the threat of high legal costs, insurers will often wish to settle before the matter comes to court – which for a combative editor who may wish to see the case through can become extremely problematic.

## Copyright

Copyright is essential to publishing – without it, publishers would not be able to make a profit from the materials they produce. Copyright law in the UK dates back to the Statute of Anne 1709, but became statutory law in 1911 with the passing of the Copyright Act, itself modified in the Copyright, Designs, Patent Act 1988. This was further modified by the Copyright and Related Rights Regulations 2003 that dealt with attempts to crack digital protection rights to make electronic copies of documents.

Beyond the UK, there is no single standard law that operates the same way in every country, but there are several international treaties that have their basis in the 1886 Berne Convention.

Copyright, as the UK Intellectual Property Office points out, is a private right that enables the creator of a work, whether produced as a written text, music, film or broadcast, to decide how it is distributed. It is in place to protect the outcome of a person's labour and, as intellectual property, can be bought and sold or transferred to a third party. This is what often happens when a publisher (whether of literature, music or film) buys the rights to a particular work.

Intellectual property rights exist independently of the work they protect and are assigned automatically. There is no official registration system in the UK (nor most of the rest of the world), although publishers in various media will often mark a work as under copyright with the symbol ©. This allows readers and other users to know that a work has entered the period of copyright, and so illegal copies cannot be made and distributed.

## Terms of copyright

To come under the terms of copyright, a work must be original. This is not the same as saying that the work has never been done before, but that it exists in a unique form. Facts or ideas themselves cannot be copyrighted, but the particular expression of these can attract copyright protection. In the UK, a single word is not sufficient to compose a work covered by copyright, although a phrase may be registered as a trade mark.

Since August 1989, after the 1988 Act came into place, copyright belongs with the author in the first instance – and not the person who commissioned the work as often was the case previously. However, for work produced as part of employment, such as by a staff writer, copyright now belongs to the employer. Freelances may be employed for a specific piece of work (a contract *for* service), which means that they own copyright unless this is specifically negotiated by the editor. Alternatively, if they work for a publisher for a period of time (a contract *of* service) then copyright for all their work done under that contract belongs to the employer, even if it is done at home.

For literary, dramatic, musical or artistic works, as well as films, the duration of the copyright is 70 years after the author's death or, if the author is unknown, 70 years after the period when it was made available to the public. Duration of copyright for sound recordings and broadcasts is 50 years from the year in which the work was made, and typographical arrangements have a duration of 25 years from the date they were created.

## Moral rights

Under the 1988 Act, an author is ascribed moral rights to a work, although this affects journalists much less than other producers, whether literary or in other media, because of certain exceptions.

Moral rights mean that the author has the right to be identified as such – a work cannot be published under another name if the author does not agree. In addition, a work cannot be modified without the author's permission, and certainly not in a derogatory way that will diminish his or her reputation.

However, because of the difficulties of producing work for magazines and newspapers to tight deadlines and with many writers, exceptions were written into the Act. Moral rights, therefore, do not apply to an employee's work, or for those made for publication in periodicals or collected reference works. Without this, anyone producing even a short news paragraph would have to receive a byline, and subs would not be able to make changes without the author's express permission.

## Fair dealing

Under copyright laws, it is an offence to copy a work, rent, lend or perform it in any way to the public, or adapt it.

However, there are conditions under which it is possible to make limited use of a work that will not infringe its rights, what is known as 'fair dealing'. Thus a work can be used for private and research study purposes, and lending for educational purposes. It is also possible to copy parts of a work when engaged in criticism and news reporting, and incidental reproductions (for example, a poster in the background of a photograph) are protected.

There are also certain other users, not relevant to print magazines, where fair dealing comes into play, such as the ability of non-profit making organisations to play sound recordings. Also, changes from 2003 made it illegal to produce copies of documents for commercial purposes (exceptions that had previously been allowed).

In practice, journalists will not be sued for copyright infringement when using quotes so long as these do not constitute a major part of their article. Conventionally, fair dealing has been taken to mean up to 400 words in one extract, or 800 words in a series of extracts (none of which should be more than 250 words individually).

## Intellectual property rights and digital media

Although not the subject of a book on print magazines in themselves, the most recent controversies around copyright relate to distribution and dissemination of material on the Internet. While the biggest problems relating to infringement of copyright have affected music publishers and film studios, with the move by a number of publishers onto the World Wide Web this does remain an area of concern.

At root, the difficulty of new technologies for publishers of traditional media is twofold. First, older means of copying (such as audio tape or photocopying), nearly always incurred an inevitable degradation between the original and the copy. With digital media, it is possible to create a perfect, or near-perfect, copy almost instantly.

Second, the distribution of different products such as video cassettes, books and printed magazines, meant that the effort of manufacturing and selling copyrighted work on a large scale was difficult. This is not the same as impossible, and indeed a big market for pirated materials remains in the distribution of illegal DVDs, for example. However, the ease with which electronic data can be passed between international borders has created difficulties for producers who wish to enforce intellectual property rights around the world, particularly in emerging markets such as China or parts of Eastern Europe.

The most strenuous responses against what has been seen as a threat from new media have been the US Digital Millennium Copyright Act (DMCA) 1998, and the EU Copyright Directive (EUCD) 2001 (implemented in the UK as the Copyright and Related Rights Regulations 2003). Each of these similar Acts placed severe restrictions upon any attempt to circumvent copyright restrictions through the use of new technologies. More recently, however, attempts have been made to reform these bills which are often seen by opponents as anti-competitive, having reduced the right of the consumer to fair use.

## Confidential information

There may be times when a journalist comes into possession of confidential information which must be handled sensitively. The basis of laws surrounding confidentiality in the UK is largely a result of judgments in common law rather than statutes passed by Parliament, although the Human Rights Act 1998, which came into effect in 2000, did give qualified rights to protect information from private life, but not if there is a threat in terms of crime or public health.

To be confidential, information must not be in the public domain in any way – so while a company may protect its trade secrets, if these have been registered for a patent then disseminating that information does not break any laws of confidentiality. Traditionally, the law of confidentiality protects personal information, government secrets and trade secrets. Usually it is information that is commercial in some degree, but can also cover material that relates to personal morality or of a sexual nature.

Outside of information unlawfully obtained, confidentiality can affect journalists in other ways. First of all, there is a question of confidential sources: sometimes a reporter will have information the source of which he or she does not want to reveal in any way. Before the Contempt of

Court Act 1981, journalists could go to prison for failing to reveal those sources when ordered by a judge, but since then a court can only require disclosure if national security is threatened.

This type of situation is very rare for magazine (as opposed to newspaper) journalists. More commonly, they may encounter information that is given to them 'off the record'. If a source does not wish to be identified, the writer should exercise caution: if journalists include non-attributable material, the motivation of the source needs to be questioned. It should also be thoroughly checked – particularly if there is a danger of publishing potentially libellous statements.

Finally, journalists may frequently be asked to sign a non-disclosure agreement (NDA), particularly if they work for a B2B magazine. This is a legal contract between a magazine and other source, usually a PR agency or company, requiring the title not to disclose certain information shared for a particular purpose.

Typically, a company will have a new product or service that they wish to reveal to the public at a particular time. Under such circumstances they may approach several publications and provide advance information that is not to be published before a certain date. Often they will contain a penalty clause, outlining the compensation that will be paid if there is a breach of confidence.

## Data protection and freedom of information

With the passing of the Data Protection Act 1988, certain types of information have been given statutory protection in the UK. It relates to personal information, rather than trade or government secrets, and applies across all types of businesses, not just magazines.

Under the Act, individuals have a wide range of rights, including access to any information held about them, the right to correct that information, protection from unsolicited marketing, and the ability to claim compensation. It does not protect individual privacy at all costs, but does try to balance those needs against the often legitimate requirements of a company or organisation to hold information.

For magazines, data protection often affects other departments more than editorial, in that as a company a publication will collect considerable amounts of data of a personal nature on subscribers and readers. As such, a magazine must be sure that anyone it collects information from is aware of why and how that data is held, and ensure that it is correct and up to date.

Once such information is no longer reasonably usable (for example, in the case of subscribers who have cancelled and no longer wish to purchase a title), it should be destroyed. There are also strict limits placed on what can be done with this information in terms of selling it to third parties. The Act is regulated by the Information Commissioner's Office.

Another law affecting the use of information is the Freedom of Information (FOI) Act 2000, which gives people access to information held by public bodies (a separate Act was passed for Scotland in 2002). Previously, government information was often closed off to the public for a standard 30-year period, but now it is considered open from the start unless exemptions apply. These exemptions include issues of national security, law enforcement and investigations by public authorities among other things.

Those wishing to discover information held in the National Archive or in departmental bodies do so by sending a written request (letter, fax or email) to the FOI authority. If they are not happy with the response, they can complain to the Information Commissioner's Office as the independent regulator of the Act.

## Privacy

In contrast to relatively clear laws governing the communication of data, there is no law that protects an individual's privacy as it would commonly be understood when intruded upon by the media. Despite some high-profile cases in recent years, such as those of Catherine Zeta Jones and Michael Douglas against *Hello!* in 2003 and an award to the Radio 1 presenter Sara Cox (actually settled out of court) that may, in the words of one judge, be creating a privacy law 'bit by bit', there is still no overarching law protecting personal privacy.

In 1995, a House of Commons Select Committee had recommended that should such a law exist, it would protect personal information and also preserve a person from harassment. The first part has, to a lesser or greater extent, been covered by data protection laws, but the latter is still largely governed by self-regulation rather than legislation. The Human Rights Act, however, does give protection to some areas of private and family life.

The most recent version of the Press Complaints Commission (PCC) Code of Practice, ratified in August 2007, states under clause 3 on Privacy that: 'Editors will be expected to justify intrusions into any individual's private life without consent.' In addition, it states that photographs should not be taken of individuals in private places without their consent, and (in clause 4 under the heading Harassment) that 'Journalists must not engage in intimidation, harassment or persistent pursuit'.

However, there are a number of clauses in the code to which there may be exceptions where the breach of the code can be demonstrated to be in the public interest, and so complaints to the PCC are not always upheld.

Stories held to be in the public interest include: those in which a crime or serious impropriety may be exposed; where public health and safety needs to be protected; and where the public needs to be protected from being misled by an individual or organisation. In addition, there is a very wide-ranging exception in that the code states: 'There is a public interest in freedom of expression itself.'

Where there is an appeal to public interest, the PCC expects a publication to demonstrate how that interest was fulfilled. In such cases, journalists have to take into account when a private person becomes a public figure. Celebrities, politicians and members of the royal family are clearly open to public scrutiny, although even in those cases the PCC may uphold complaints when a publication has failed to take into account their right to a private life.

However, the issue can become more vexed when dealing with individuals who do not court publicity in any way, but whose daily activities (for example, as part of their profession) may lead journalists to inquire – or intrude – into their private lives. Many of the complaints upheld by the PCC when dealing with such people are usually directed at newspapers, especially the regional press. However, it is noteworthy that the recent increase in real-life story magazines, such as *Chat*, has resulted in an increase in complaints to the PCC.

## Copy approval

Piers Morgan in his diaries, *The Insider*, commented that copy approval, the practice of allowing a third party, such as an interviewee or company, the right to see information about them before it goes to print, 'is a hidden shame . . . that has grown in recent years to be an epidemic'.

The difficulty for a large number of publications, particularly tabloid newspapers and celebrity magazines, is that they need interviews with famous (or even not-so-famous) people to sell their issues, but those figures are unlikely to agree unless they can see and approve copy beforehand. Even B2B titles can find themselves in the position of having to negotiate deals with companies and organisations, and PR agencies will always wish to view copy before it is published.

It is perfectly reasonable for someone working in PR to want to view information about their client, to capitalise on good news or prepare for the worst. However, it is more than equally reasonable for an editor to refuse.

The most sensible position – if not always the easiest – is to issue a blanket refusal on all copy approval. This might result in missed 'scoops', but it will make the editorial department's job much easier in the long run: once it becomes known that a title agreed to show material prior to publication to one individual or organisation, then plenty of others will want the same privilege. Of course, when issuing such a blanket refusal there is greater responsibility on the journalist to be accurate and fair.

## Codes of conduct

As well as the threat of legal action, the practice of journalism is also subject to professional codes of conduct, ways of acting that are considered best practice. Many individual publications will issue their own codes to staff, ways of behaving at work that they feel are essential to the job, and many countries around the world (especially in Europe and North America) have long-established national codes that are adopted by journalists working in the profession.

In the UK, the National Union of Journalists provides a code of professional behaviour that may be viewed at www.nuj.org.uk. The most recent version, updated in 2007, runs as follows:

A journalist

1  At all times upholds and defends the principle of media freedom, the right of freedom of expression and the right of the public to be informed.

2  Strives to ensure that information disseminated is honestly conveyed, accurate and fair.

3  Does her/his utmost to correct harmful inaccuracies.

4  Differentiates between fact and opinion.

5  Obtains material by honest, straightforward and open means, with the exception of investigations that are both over-whelmingly in the public interest and which involve evidence that cannot be obtained by straightforward means.

6  Does nothing to intrude into anybody's private life, grief or distress unless justified by overriding consideration of the public interest.

7  Protects the identity of sources who supply information in confidence and material gathered in the course of her/his work.

8  Resists threats or any other inducements to influence, distort or suppress information.

9  Takes no unfair personal advantage of information gained in the course of her/his duties before the information is public knowledge.

10  Produces no material likely to lead to hatred or discrimination on the grounds of a person's age, gender, race, colour, creed, legal status, disability, marital status, or sexual orientation.

11  Does not by way of statement, voice or appearance endorse by advertisement any commercial product or service save for the promotion of her/his own work or of the medium by which she/he is employed.

12  Avoids plagiarism.

In addition to the NUJ code, the Press Complaints Commission issues its own code with which every journalist should be familiar, and which can be viewed at www.pcc.org.uk/cop/practice.html. This covers ethical standards to which publications and journalists should adhere if they wish to avoid censure in the areas of accuracy, the right to reply, privacy and harassment, reporting on children, reporting crime, the use of clandestine devices to obtain information, financial journalism, and payment to criminals or witnesses in criminal trials.

## Complaints and the right to reply

Sometimes a magazine can get things wrong, and sometimes a reader might feel that a magazine has got things wrong. The two are not always the same, but an editor should have a policy in place to deal with both types of complaint.

Even if a mistake has happened, this does not automatically mean that legal action can, or should, be taken. In any case, in the first instance when a complaint is received, the initial course of action should not be automatically to apologise, as this could be taken as an admission of liability. The first step, if the complainant is making contact via phone, is to take notes but also to ask them to confirm the complaint in writing. After this, the editor should go about collecting relevant information about the article in question, such as any interviews, emails or other documents.

Once a complaint has been received in writing, then it must be addressed more formally. Again, the automatic route should not be simply to issue an apology either by letter or print, but to determine what the facts of the case are. If a claim is without substance, then the editor has to stand firm: to do otherwise could itself prompt further demands and even claims of libel.

If the magazine is in error, then the next step may be to publish a correction or apology. Attempts to be reasonable can be helpful in a court case, but of themselves they do not remove the need for a suit if, for example, the complainant believes that he or she has been libelled.

When publishing a correction or apology, this does need to be seen and agreed by the complainant. A condition of publication should be that the complainant will also provide a written statement accepting the apology as full and final settlement. If an editor or publisher has to engage in communication with the complainant in cases that are likely to become aggravated, then letters are best sent through a lawyer and marked clearly 'without prejudice', so that they cannot be used as evidence in a legal action.

While the gravest concern of an editor must be lawsuits that could be very costly, there will be plenty of other times when a magazine is approached with complaints that have less serious consequences but need to be handled sensitively. Plenty of readers will want to complain to the editor when they do not receive their subscription, for example, but such details have to be passed on to the appropriate department. Likewise, the prevalence of readers' pages is a good opportunity to demonstrate a magazine's ability to respond to the needs of its readers, as a sounding board for things they do not like as well as those they do.

# 8
# Conclusion
## The future of magazines

This book is primarily concerned with print magazines. In the words of Mark Glaser (2005), 'the magazine world has seen the future of print – and it's still print', and any predictions that the Internet would replace print are unlikely to be true in the immediate future. Although magazine publishing saw a fall shortly after 2000, as part of a general economic downturn in the wake of the bursting of the dotcom bubble, more recently it has been buoyant. September 2007 saw publication of the largest ever consumer magazine, as an edition of *Vogue* went on sale with 840 pages, 727 of which were filled with advertising.

The simple fact is that print works, and innovations in technology and printing, such as the competition stimulated by the introduction of Adobe's InDesign, or the increasingly widespread use of PDF and computer to plate printing, indicate that print magazine production has a long future. Nonetheless, the growth of the Internet, particularly the web, has opened up a huge number of possibilities (and not a few headaches) for magazine publishers and editors.

## Magazines and the web

At the end of the 1990s, with the rapid growth of online use that had taken place since the invention of the World Wide Web – and the even more rapid inflation of hyperbole that accompanied dotcom investments – many punters were predicting the end of traditional print media. Here was a medium the distribution of which was truly international, which could be customised in new and exciting ways by consumers, and which would drastically cut the costs of getting information to the public.

Yet the new medium also brought with it a host of other problems. Since the early years of the Internet, users had benefited from the custom of obtaining data for free: any online publication that attempted to charge for a subscription simply saw readers go elsewhere. Of course, that left advertising – but many of the early claims to online advertisers, that this would prove the perfect opportunity to track potential buyers through to the final sale, proved to be unfounded and over-hyped. What is more, the notion that the Net could provide virtually free distribution of data neglected to take into account the costs of bandwidth and creating content specific to the web – rather than shovelling on articles created for other media.

In the end, the plain truism is that people use different media in different ways. Readers who are more than happy to peruse page after page of features in a glossy magazine are not willing to do the same online. While newspapers have suffered at the hands of the web (although some of this is also due to the fact that many chose to increase cover prices and willingly sacrificed readers to increase revenue), the nature of good news writing – where relevant information can be gleaned at the top of the story – makes it ideal for online publications. The same is not true for longer articles or reviews.

People do use the Internet more, and to do this they have to give up some of the time they spent consuming more traditional media. The types of sites that are popular, however – news sites, search engines and portals, forums, social networking sites such as Facebook – often operate very differently to the newspapers, television and magazines that were the main options open to them before.

This draws attention to the first feature of transferring magazines online: by and large shovelware does not work. This is mainly because there will always be a few people who want to access features from a magazine online, but most readers will not be happy going from page to page onscreen.

Magazines that want a significant online presence have to think of new ways to engage with readers. In many cases, this will be to provide some kind of interaction that is not easily available in a weekly or monthly periodical. The ideal is that the magazine drives readers to the web site, while the web site, in turn, drives some of its visitors back to the magazine.

Most national titles now have some form of online presence, although in some cases, particularly for consumer titles, this largely consists of window dressing that advertises the print publication. However, and this is especially the case in the B2B sector, web publishing has become an important add-on to print, offering daily news and interactive forums that allow editors and journalists to engage in new and exciting ways with their readers.

## Online magazines

Serious web publishing is little more than ten years old, the original trailblazers being Time Inc. Magazines and *Wired*, which both began experimenting with the new medium in 1994. In that time online magazines have gone from the sublime to the ridiculous and, finally, appear to be approaching a degree of maturity.

One example of the ridiculously sublime was the immense amounts of money that were thrown at 'content providers' (or, among other things, journalists as they used to be known) for a brief period during the dotcom boom. This was followed by a period of sublime ridicule when plenty of contributors were expected to work, more or less, for nothing as publishers cut back in the face of negligible advertising revenues.

Today, while there has been a clear-out of many online magazines – and there are very few online-*only* publications, *Slate* and *Salon* being notable exceptions – those that remain are finally beginning to become quite profitable and useful additions to a title's stable. Sites such as those for *Newsweek*, *The Wall Street Journal* and *New Scientist* attract significant numbers of visitors each day and, as well as providing information in innovative ways, can also be very profitable.

As well as the extension of existing magazines onto the web, there is also the 'magazinification' of other very popular sites. Thus portals such as MSN and Yahoo! regularly include articles on a range of topics, from dating to handling your finances, which would not look out of place in the consumer press and draw upon the styles and presentation of popular magazines.

## The role of the online editor

For publications that have a serious web presence, an online editor may have as many responsibilities as the print editor. He or she will be expected to liaise with the publisher and sales team, as well as oversee editorial and graphic design departments. For smaller concerns, the print editor may also take charge of the web site, and in any case it is most likely that the online editor will report to the main magazine editor.

Here we shall concentrate on those elements that will probably be different to the role of a print editor, while noting that many of the tasks and responsibilities pointed out in Chapters 4 to 6 concerning editorial, art and production will also apply.

One significant difference is in terms of deadlines and the timescale of a web site. A web site in some ways is closer to a newspaper than a magazine in that visitors will expect to see content updated on a daily basis. Indeed, daily updates may not be enough, with journalists expected to contribute throughout the day as and when news becomes available, making an online publication more like a broadcast newsroom.

Once the technical infrastructure is in place (a server capable of dealing with thousands of page hits and shifting megabytes, or even gigabytes of data per hour), publishing to the web is much simpler than sending to print, although the cost of constant technical support and maintenance should not be underestimated. In recent years, the fundamental principles of good web design have separated content (such as words and images or video) from the structure of a web site, how content is presented in a particular format to the end user, and its design, the look and feel of a page.

Professional web sites will now be dynamic, information stored in one or more databases that can be accessed by different types of page for different platforms, which is why separating structure and design from content is so important. If your reader is accessing a page from a mobile phone or digital television, their experience will be very different to that of someone who views the same information on a PC.

While many sites appear to have hundreds or even thousands of pages of content, in terms of design there will only be a few templates that strip out information from a database and present it to the reader. The virtue of this approach is that it makes it incredibly easy to redesign the whole site. In addition, it means that writers can concentrate on what they are good at – writing – entering their text into some form of content management system (see below) and leaving final presentation of their content in the more capable hands of the designer who set up the original system.

In addition to overseeing the production cycle, then, which will result in content being uploaded on a daily basis for some sections, less often for others, the online editor will also have to consider ways to interact with readers on site. Interaction is key to what is often referred to as 'sticky' content, and increasingly web sites are becoming reliant on their visitors providing them with much of the original material that they use.

## Convergent media

A key term when dealing with new media is *convergence*. In terms of communication theory, this is the notion that new technologies will bring about the merger of every mass medium into one, but in everyday terms it means that magazine publishers now have to think of formats that were previously the preserve of broadcasters when publishing online.

In one sense, magazines have demonstrated a mastery of one type of convergence – that of text and image – for the past century or more, and some of the design skills that made magazines popular in the twentieth century are now being applied to online media in the twenty-first.

This said, the key distinction between print and online versions of magazines is that it is unwise to rely on text as heavily on screen as on the page. This is not to diminish the role of text – in many cases there is no better way to convey information clearly and concisely than through the written word.

Yet the virtues of audio and video as part of a multimedia website cannot be neglected. Many sites such as *New Scientist, .Net* and *BBC History Magazine* offer regular podcasts for visitors (some only available to subscribers to the site) where they can catch up with regular audio bulletins, or radio-style features that provide an insight into particular issues of interest to the audience. What is more, the spread of broadband in the past five years or so means that for the first time streaming audio and video is usable to more visitors than ever before.

At its simplest, a podcast may be an audio file in a format such as MP3 that can be clicked on and downloaded to a computer or player. More complex forms of podcasting will involve a 'feed', whereby the listener subscribes to an RSS (really simple syndication) service that announces when files are available: rather than 'pulling' them to his or her computer, that is visiting a web site and clicking a link, subscribed feeds will be 'pushed' directly to the computer.

In addition to audio, titles such as *Time* and *Stuff* magazines are starting to use video in interesting ways. Video podcasting, often shortened to vidcasting or vodcasting, works in a similar way to audio podcasting, with short-format news or feature videos available via feeds or simply by clicking on a link. The YouTube phenomenon, whereby users upload videos to the web for others to view around the world, has greatly improved the popularity of this format in recent years.

## Content management and multi-platform publishing

The division of labour that takes place on modern commercial web sites will be familiar to many who work in magazines, and is roughly analogous to the split between editorial, art/design, and production/printing. Because of the demands of fast deadlines and high turnover of articles, a professional site will make use of some form of content management system (CMS).

A CMS allows a potentially large number of users to add multimedia elements – whether text, images, audio or video – to a web site as easily as possible. As well as being the primary source of generating content, a CMS enables files to be shared in a non-proprietary format, so that those files can be opened by as many people as possible, and is also used for archiving purposes, automatically saving old editions of an online magazine, for example, so that they can be searched quickly and simply.

CMS may be developed in-house, such as the system used by Emap Interactive, or it may be used on freely available, open-source software such as Joomla! (www.joomla.org) or Mambo (www.mamboserver.com). Any CMS should enable journalists to upload content such as news stories or images quickly via a browser, and will include tools for editing online (such as holding stories in reserve until they have been subbed and agreed by an editor).

The more advanced content management systems will even include tools to manage such things as blogs, wikis and e-commerce (so that visitors to a site can purchase merchandise). Nearly all will include planning tools, so that editorial calendars and schedules can be managed efficiently, as well as having built-in banner services to deal with banner advertising on web sites.

While the techniques of designing and writing for the web are different to those for print, contemporary designers and journalists need to be flexible to work across both. What's more, while shovelware is a very poor way to create a web site in that content designed for print is rarely the appropriate format online, publishing companies will generate a huge amount of material, some of which is ultimately to be used across very different platforms – whether the printed page, a computer web site or, increasingly, a mobile phone.

Another important part of content management is what is often referred to as digital asset management. A magazine will originate text documents, photos, illustrations, and even videos and audio as part of its online content, that needs to be stored, catalogued and annotated so that it can be quickly called up and transferred to the right place.

Multi-platform publishing has become much more important to companies such as Adobe. Its acquisition of Macromedia, a company specialising in multimedia web design, in 2005, is one reason why InDesign has started to become the popular choice for a number of publishers. As well as offering streamlined tools for publishing in print via PDF, each version of its Creative Suite includes more options to manage assets for both print and the web.

## Forums, wikis and blogs

Another use of technology is not simply to get content to an audience in as sophisticated a manner as possible, but to encourage interaction with that audience in ways that simply are not possible via print. Many magazines will have such things as letters pages, and readers will be able to contact editorial staff via phone and email, but an exciting possibility offered by new media and the Internet is the ability to engage in dialogue with those readers in a more immediate fashion.

An online editor will find that this is one of his or her most important tasks, to provide a community for magazine readers where they can interact with members of staff on a daily basis. Indeed, for a successful site it is often the case that such things as forums, blogs and wikis generate more visits than 'official' content based on the articles that appear in a magazine.

The longest-serving form of interactivity is the forum, where visitors can leave messages for the editors and journalists or even other readers. This is the opportunity to pass comment on the magazine, ask for help that is relevant to the area served by the publication and, perhaps, direct visitors to other sites of interest on the web.

Of course, such interactive content can bring its own dangers. In contrast to a professionally trained team of journalists, most members of the public have only the vaguest idea of issues such as libel, which has led many publishers and editors to be wary of engaging in this type of content. In 2007, a series of defamatory postings on the parenting web site Mumsnet.com led the owners of the site to settle out of court with a parenting expert.

Despite these dangers, the courts do seem to be recognising the difficulties inherent in such use of media and, as long as a forum is moderated properly and establishes a clear policy to handle potentially defamatory postings (as well as other contentious material, such as that where the copyright is held elsewhere), this can be an extremely rewarding way to engage with the audience.

Other options to provide new material in an innovative format is via blogs and wikis. An increasing number of sites include blogs (or web logs) with regular postings from an editor or staff writer. Blogging is an easy way to combine text, images and other multimedia elements – so that journalists visiting a trade show, for example, can upload their digital snaps from the event. It is somewhat more informal than the traditional journalistic route of printing finished articles, offering instead a diary format for readers to follow new developments.

An added advantage of blogging is the ability to post comments or links to an article. This turns the process into a sort of forum where readers can provide instant feedback or their own additional information.

Added to this, although a format only just beginning to be exploited by professional journalists, is the wiki, a database where any user with access can edit the content. The most famous example, of course, is Wikipedia, but Paul Bradshaw of the Online Journalism Blog (onlinejournalismblog. wordpress.com) has described wiki journalism as the new blogs. Some wikis are simply a means of sharing information between an editorial team, but they also provide the opportunity to engage in new types of journalism, for example, what Bradshaw calls 'crowdsourcing' where material can be produced that would be impossible for in-house staff to cover due to logistical reasons.

These and other technological developments, often grouped together under the label 'Web 2.0', indicate some of the ways in which all sorts of media, including magazines, will develop in the coming years. Print is far from dead, but the ability for what was traditionally considered the passive audience to generate content more easily than ever before constitutes a revolution in the ways we all deal with the media. The technology of magazines may extend backwards more than 300 years, but the production process which brings together different media, edited and handled by professionals used to dealing with tight deadlines and potentially difficult subjects, means that magazine journalism also has a long future.

# Glossary

**ABC:** Audit Bureau of Circulation, with the BPA one of the main bodies that verifies how many copies of a title are distributed.

**Advertorial:** Advertising feature designed to look like editorial. Also known as an advertising feature.

**Affinity sales:** Magazines sold in specialist shops that are sympathetic to the title, for example, a music magazine in a music store.

**Audit:** An independent check by a body such as ABC or BPA to verify copies in circulation.

**Average net circulation:** The average number of copies produced per issue, which may be measured as paid net circulation (that is copies sold).

**B2B:** Business-to-business, professional titles formerly known as trade magazines aimed at a specific industry.

**Bar code:** The machine readable strip of bars on a cover that contains information such as price and title.

**Bimonthly/biweekly:** A magazine published once every two months or two weeks.

**Binding:** Means of fastening pages together, typically saddle-stitch (stapling) or perfect (glue).

**Bit map:** An image described as a series of coloured pixels on screen.

**Bleed:** Printing beyond the boundary of the page so that, once it is trimmed, ink goes right to the edge of the page.

**Body copy:** The main text of a page.

**BPA:** Business Publications Audit, along with ABC the main organisation that verifies magazine circulation.

**BRAD:** British Rates and Data, monthly publication that lists newspaper and magazine titles in the UK.

**Brief:** The summary of what an article should consist of when commissioned by an editor.

**Bulk sales:** Discounted copies that are sold in bulk to a company, such as a hotel or airline, that often gives them free to customers.

**Bureau:** An external company used to prepare films from digital files.

**Byline:** Journalist's name given with an article.

**Camera ready copy:** A layout ready to be photographed to make plates.

**Caption:** Text associated with a picture and providing additional information.

**Centre spread:** Centre pages of a saddle-stitched magazine.

**Churn:** The rate of turnover in subscribers each year.

**Classified advertising:** Advertising sold by the column or centimetre, as opposed to display advertising sold by the page.

**Close:** To finish production and send the magazine to the printers.

**CMYK:** Cyan, magenta, yellow and black, the four inks typically used in full-colour printing.

**Colour proof:** A high-quality representation of how a page will look once printed.

**Colour separation:** The four plates of CMYK ink used to create a full-colour print.

**Commissioning:** The process of hiring a freelance writer or artist to produce content for a magazine.

**Consumer magazines:** Titles aimed at the general public, as opposed to B2B or specialist publications.

**Contract publishing:** Publishing magazines for a third party.

**Controlled circulation:** Distribution of a magazine free to specified individuals, for example, those working in a particular industry.

**Copyright:** The legal ownership of creative work.

**Cover mount:** Free gift attached to the front of a magazine.

**CPM:** Cost per mil (sometimes mille), or cost per thousand: the cost of reaching a thousand readers or advertisers with a page or publication.

**Cromalin:** Brand name for one type of colour proof.

**CTP:** Computer to plate, creating a plate using a laser to remove the need for film.

**Defamation:** A statement that will harm the reputation of another person.

**Demographic:** Information about a magazine audience, including such things as age, income and socio-economic status (ABC1/C2DE).

**Direct to plate:** Another way of referring to CTP.

**Display advertising:** Advertising sold by the page rather than column centimetres.

**Distributor:** Company responsible for getting a magazine from the printer to the consumer, whether via a store or via subscription.

**DPI:** Dots per inch, a way of measuring the resolution of scanners and printers.

**DPS:** Double-page spread, feature or advertising over two pages.

**Drop cap:** Initial letter at the beginning of an article or paragraph that is larger than the surrounding text.

**DTP:** Desktop Publishing, software used to lay out pages on computer.

**Dummy:** Mock-up of a magazine produced to test how it will be received.

**Ed/ad ratio:** The ratio of editorial pages to advertising.

**Editor:** Person in charge of a magazine or section of a magazine.

**Editorial:** Material produced by journalists working for the magazine, but also articles expressing the opinion of the editor or publication.

**Editorial assistant:** Someone who provides support for the editorial staff, such as answering phones and checking that invoices are submitted to the finance department.

**EPoS:** Electronic Point of Sale, information stored on computer whenever an item is sold.

**E-zine:** Electronic magazine, usually on the web.

**Facing matter:** Advertising that faces appropriate editorial.

**Fair comment:** A defence against certain libel actions.

**Fair use:** The ability to copy a certain amount of material without permission from the copyright holder.

**Film:** A photographic representation of a page, usually on acetate, that is used to make printing plates.

**Firm sale:** Titles paid for and not returnable.

**Flat-plan:** A map of a magazine issue that shows where editorial and advertising pages will appear.

**Font:** A set of characters, different sizes and styles.

**Footer:** Information at the bottom of a page.

**Format:** The size and shape of a page, such as A4.

**Gatefold:** A page, usually inside the cover, that opens out to accommodate extra advertising.

**Gone to bed:** When a magazine is at the printers and cannot be modified.

**Grid:** The underlying structure of a page design that determines the position of such things as columns and pictures.

**Gutter:** The blank space between facing pages of a publication.

**Hard copy:** Text on paper rather than screen.

**Header:** Information at the top of a page.

**House ad:** Advertisement placed in a magazine by the publisher rather than external advertiser.

**House style:** The set of rules that determines such things as spellings for disputed words, punctuation and use of numerals.

**ICC:** International Colour Consortium, body that governs standards for colour processing and printing.

**Indent:** Text placed further away from the edge of the page than other copy, leaving white space.

**InDesign:** Standard page layout package used to produce magazines.

**Insert:** Loose advertising or other material that is inserted between magazine pages.

**ISSN:** International Standard Serial Number, a unique number assigned to every magazine.

**JPEG:** File format used for digital images.

**Justification:** The alignment of text on one or both sides of a column or page.

**Kerning:** Moving letters closer together so that they fit more neatly.

**Kill fee:** Payment made for an article that is not used.

**Layout:** The design of a page, combining text and graphical elements.

**Leading:** The vertical space between lines of type.

**Libel:** A published statement that is defamatory.

**Listings:** Brief details of events.

**Literal:** A spelling mistake.

**Lithography:** The underlying technology behind most printing. Originally printing via stone (hence litho), but now usually metal and sometimes plastic plates.

**Lower case:** Text that is not capitalised.

**LPI:** Lines per inch, the measure of resolution of film, as opposed to DPI.

**Malicious falsehood:** Defamatory statement against products rather than individuals or organisations.

**Masthead:** The title of a magazine.

**Matchprint:** Brand name of a colour proofing system.

**Mechanical data:** Information about page sizes, bleed and trim sizes.

**Media pack:** Information about a magazine's brand, its readers and advertising rates for potential advertisers.

**Model-release form:** Agreement signed by a photographer's model, allowing the magazine to use the image.

**Net paid circulation:** Total circulation for all copies of a magazine, where the consumer pays at least half the cover price.

**Newsletter:** Publication with basic production values and distributed via subscription.

**NRS:** National Readership Survey, organisation that conducts demographic research for publications in the UK.

**Off the record:** A statement made with restrictions as to how it can be reported or attributed.

**Offset litho printing:** The main technique of printing, where ink from a metal plate is transferred to a rubber sheet before being printed onto paper.

**On spec:** Material offered to an editor that has not been commissioned, on the chance that it might be used.

**Overheads:** Publishing costs not directly related to the business of magazine production.

**Overrun:** Additional copies of an issue above the set print run.

**Page rate:** The cost for taking out a page of advertising in a magazine.

**Page yield:** Revenues made from advertising sold on page.

**Part work:** A magazine designed to be collected over a series of issues.

**PCC:** Press Complaints Commission, a self-regulatory body dealing with ethical issues in the UK press.

**PDF:** Portable Document Format, a file format for distributing files digitally and much used in printing.

**Perfect binding:** Pages cut and glued together to form a spine.

**Plate:** The metal (sometimes plastic) sheet that carries an image of a page and is inked for printing.

**Point of sale material:** Promotional materials used to attract consumers where a magazine is sold.

**Post-mortem:** The meeting after a magazine has been printed, to discuss what worked and what did not.

**Postscript:** Computer language describing elements of a page for printing.

**PPA:** Periodical Publishers Association, the main industry body representing magazines in the UK.

**Pre-flight:** Process of checking a file for any potential errors before it is sent to the printer.

**Print run:** The total number of copies printed for an issue.

**Proof:** A copy of a page used to check that information is accurate before printing.

**PTC:** Periodicals Training Council

**Publisher:** The person responsible for the business side and profitability of a magazine.

**QuarkXPress:** Popular page layout software.

**Rate card:** Information showing how much it costs to advertise in a magazine and including other mechanical data.

**Reach:** The percentage of a target audience reading a magazine or advertisement.

**Readership:** People who read a magazine as opposed to those who actively buy it.

**Registration:** The correct alignment of the four plates used in colour printing.

**Renewal rate:** The number of readers who renew their subscription.

**Repro:** Reproduction, the film and plate-making process of production.

**RIP:** Raster Image Processor, a machine that converts digital data into film as part of the repro process.

**Saddle-stitch binding:** Originally sewn binding, but a magazine bound by stapling.

**Spot colour:** A single colour in addition to black.

**Standfirst:** Introductory text following the title of an article.

**Strapline:** A heading just above or below another heading.

**Style sheet:** In DTP a series of formatting options that can be applied to such things as text and paragraphs.

**Sub:** A sub-editor, or shorthand for a subscription.

**Supplement:** A one-off magazine or magazine published as part of a newspaper.

**TIFF:** Image file format used for graphics.

**TMAP:** Teen Magazine Arbitration Panel, a self-regulatory body dealing with teenage magazines.

**Trim marks:** Crosses on the page showing the printer where the page should be cut after printing.

**Typeface:** Complete set of characters in a particular design.

**Web offset printing:** A common form of printing where paper is fed from huge rolls, or webs.

**White space:** Use of white space around images or text to enhance design.

# Bibliography

Benwell, B. (2003) *Masculinity and Men's Lifestyle Magazines*, Oxford: Blackwell Publishing

Bourdieu, P. (1986) 'The Forms of Capital', in J.G. Richardson (ed.), *The Handbook of Theory: Research for the Sociology of Education* (pp. 241–58), New York: Greenwood Press

Butler, J., Holden, K. and Lidwell, W. (2007) *Universal Principles of Design*, Beverly, MA: Rockport Publishers

Conboy, M. (2004) *Journalism: A Critical History*, London: Sage

Crowley, D. (2006) *Magazine Covers*, second edition, London: Mitchell Beazley

Daly, C.P., Patrick, H. and Ryder, E. (1997) *The Magazine Publishing Industry*, Needham Heights, MA: Allyn and Bacon

Elam, K. (2004) *Grid Systems: Principles of Organizing Type*, New York: Princeton Architectural Press

Fletcher, A. (2001) *The Art of Looking Sideways*, London: Phaidon

Fletcher, K. (2005) *The Journalist's Handbook*, Basingstoke: Macmillan

Franklin, B., Hamer, M., Hanna, M., Kinsey, M. and Richardson, J. (2005) *Key Concepts in Journalism*, London: Sage

Frost, C. (2001) *Reporting for Journalists*, London: Routledge

Frost, C. (2003) *Designing for Newspapers and Magazines*, London: Routledge

Gatter, M. (2005) *Getting it Right: Digital Pre-Press for Designers*, London: Laurence King Publishing

Gauntlett, D. (2002) *Media, Gender and Identity: An Introduction*, London: Routledge

Glaser, M. (2005), 'Future of Magazines: Net Could Empower Readers', www.ojr.org/ojr/stories/050524glaser

Gough-Yates, A. (2002), *Understanding Women's Magazines*, London: Routledge

Hamilton, N. (2007) *Magazine Writing*, London: Longman

Harcup, T. (2003) *Journalism: Principles and Practice*, London: Sage

Hennessy, B. (2005) *Writing Feature Articles*, fourth edition, St Louis, MO: Focal Press

Hermes, J. (1995) *Reading Women's Magazines: An Analysis of Everyday Media Use*, London: Polity Press

Hicks, W. (2002) *Subediting for Journalists*, London: Routledge

Hicks, W. (2006) *English for Journalists*, second edition, London: Routledge

Hicks, W. and Adams, S. (2001) *Interviewing for Journalists*, London: Routledge

Hicks, W., Adams, S. and Gilbert, H. (1999) *Writing for Journalists*, London: Routledge

Hutchison, E.R. (2007) *Art of Feature Writing: From Newspaper Features and Magazine Articles to Commentary*, Oxford: Oxford University Press

Jackson, P. and Stevenson, N. (2001) *Making Sense of Men's Magazines*, London: Polity Press

Johnson, S. and Prijatel, P. (1999) *Magazine Publishing*, London: McGraw-Hill

Johnson, S. and Prijatel, P. (2006) *The Magazine from Cover to Cover*, second edition, Oxford: Oxford University Press

King, S. (2001) *Magazine Designs that Work*, Beverly, MA: Rockport Publishers

Lanson, J. and Stephens, M. (2007) *Writing and Reporting the News*, third edition, Oxford: Oxford University Press

Leslie, J. (2003) *Magculture: New Magazine Design*, London: Laurence King Publishing

Lupton, E. (2004) *Thinking with Type: A Critical Guide for Designers, Writers, Editors, and Students*, New York: Princeton Architectural Press

McCracken, E. (1992) *Decoding Women's Magazines: From 'Mademoiselle' to 'Ms'*, Basingstoke: Palgrave Macmillan

McKane, A. (2004) *Journalism: A Career Handbook*, London: A & C Black

McKay, J. (2004) *The Magazines Handbook*, second edition, London: Routledge

McLoughlin, L. (2000) *The Language of Magazines*, London: Routledge

McNair, B. (2003) *News and Journalism in the UK*, fourth edition, London: Routledge

Marr, A. (2005) *My Trade: A Short History of British Journalism*, London: Pan

Mason, P. and Smith, D. (1998) *Magazine Law: A Practical Guide*, London: Routledge

Morrish, J. (2003) *Magazine Editing: How to Develop and Manage a Successful Publication*, second edition, London: Routledge

Pelusy, M. and Pelusy, J. (2005) *The Media: Magazines*, New York: Chelsea House Publishers

Phillips, A. (2006) *Good Writing for Journalists*, London: Sage

Randall, D. (2000) *The Universal Journalist*, second edition, London: Pluto Press

Renard, D. (2006) *The Last Magazine: Magazines in Transition*, New York: Universe Publishing

Rivers, C. (2006) *Mag-art: Innovation in Magazine Design and Packaging*, Hove: Rotovision

Rocha, T. (2000) *Magazine Publishing*, New York: Rosen Publishing

Samara, T. (2005) *Making and Breaking the Grid: A Layout Design Workshop*, Beverly, MA: Rockport Publishers

Strunk, W. (1999) *The Elements of Style*, fourth edition, London: Longman

Taylor, S. and Brody, N. (2006) *100 Years of Magazine Covers*, London: Black Dog Publishing

Welsh, T., Greenwood, W. and Banks, D. (2007) *McNae's Essential Law for Journalists*, eighteenth edition, Oxford: Oxford University Press

White, J.V. (2003) *Editing by Design: For Designers, Art Directors and Editors, the Classic Guide to Winning Readers*, third edition, New York: Allworth Press

Yopp, J.J. and McAdams, K.C. (2006) *Reaching Audiences: A Guide to Media Writing*, Needham Heights, MA: Allyn and Bacon

## Useful web sites

Audit Bureau of Circulations – www.abc.org.uk

Business Publications Audit – www.bpaww.com

Magforum – www.magforum.com

National Union of Journalists – www.nuj.org.uk

Pass4Press – www.pass4press.com

Periodical Publishers Association – www.ppa.co.uk

Press Complaints Commission – www.pcc.org.uk

Online Journalism Review – www.ojr.org

UK Publishing Media – www.publishingmedia.org.uk

# Index